The FORTIES

GOOD TIMES JUST AROUND THE CORNER

The FORTIES

GOOD TIMES JUST AROUND THE CORNER

Alison Maloney

First published in Great Britain in 2005 by
Michael O'Mara Books Limited
9 Lion Yard
Tremadoc Road
London SW4 7NQ

A CIP catalogue record for this book is available from
the British Library

ISBN: 978-1-84317-145-4

5 7 9 10 8 6

Designed and typeset by Design 23

Printed and bound in Singapore by Tien Wah Press

Dedication

For Nan
Alison Maloney, 2005

CONTENTS

INTRODUCTION

The 1940s, more than any other decade, can be split into two halves. As the decade dawned Britain was already three months into a war that would dominate the first half, while the second saw a nation in recovery. But when the two halves are examined as a whole, it is the amazing resourcefulness of a nation under pressure which defines the era.

Although many had already lived through World War I, the Second World War was to have a greater effect on the everyday life of the British population, not just those who were involved in the fighting.

As Winston Churchill said, in 1940, 'The whole of the warring nations are engaged, not only soldiers, but the entire population – men, women and children. The fronts are everywhere. The trenches are dug in the towns and streets. Every village is fortified. Every road is barred. The front line runs through the factories. The workmen are soldiers with different weapons but the same courage.' Every aspect of domestic life was altered, some for ever, and not a single citizen of the UK would remain untouched by the conflict in Europe.

Life under the ration book was far from easy, during and after the war and, with many men away, women were forced to be workers, as well as housewives and mothers – finding ways to feed families on a fraction of the food available to shoppers today, queuing for hours in shops and mending worn-out clothes.

For city dwellers there was also the Blitz, with the constant threat of bombing raids, to contend

THE FORTIES
Good Times Just Around The Corner

Left: Winston Churchill's wartime speeches inspired the nation.
Above: Families had to learn how to adapt to life under the ration book.

with and many had to live apart from their evacuated children. Men who were not at war spent their days at work and their nights patrolling the streets, either as air-raid wardens or members of the Home Guard. Anti-aircraft guns and air-raid sirens became the nightly norm and many nights were spent sleeping on makeshift beds or floors in air-raid shelters and, in London, Underground stations.

The blackout meant that everyone was forced to block up their windows with wood or blackout curtains, in an attempt to hide highly populated areas from the enemy aircraft above, and the cry of 'Put that light out!' from air-raid wardens echoed through the city streets. Road signs were removed so that, should an enemy invasion occur, the attacking forces wouldn't know which way to go – although this merely resulted in Brits getting lost a lot! Iron railings were requisitioned to make munitions and women donated pots and pans to help with the war effort.

There was some fun to be had in the forties too. Cinema was booming, with classic films such

urged civilians to 'Dig For Victory', 'Make Do and Mend', 'Careless Talk Costs Lives' and 'Be like Dad, Keep Mum'. Advertisers got in on the act too, with a poster for New Berry Fruits proclaiming them 'The Fruits of Victory' and a draper's shop in Bromley, Kent, advertising balaclavas and wool mufflers as 'Comforts for your fighting men.'

The decade brought about major social change with women finding that they could go out to work, the birth of the 'teenager' as a social group and a shift in attitudes towards child-rearing which followed the publication of Dr Spock's *Common Sense Book of Baby and Child Care*.

The war also brought about a change in international attitudes with the formation of the United Nations, which has been attempting to stop world conflict and deal with its after-effects ever since.

But above all else, the 1940s showed how a nation could pull together in times of trouble and, in the words of one famous Vera Lynn hit 'Keep smiling through'.

Left: A Civil Defence volunteer assesses bomb damage in London.
Above: This post-war booklet explained the purpose of the new United Nations.
Right: Propaganda posters like this warned against wasting food.

as *Gone with the Wind* and *The Third Man* hitting screens, while the music scene was being modernized with a new dance craze from America and dance halls full to bursting every Saturday night. At home, entertainment was provided by the radio, with a mixture of comedy programmes, like *ITMA,* and uplifting songs such as 'We'll Meet Again' and 'Run Rabbit Run' fortifying the collective spirit.

Technological advances included the ballpoint pen, terylene, microwave ovens and disposable nappies.

It was a time of slogans. The phrase 'Don't you know there's a war on?' became a mantra. Posters

WASTE THE FOOD AND HELP THE HUN

CHAPTER ONE

THE FORTIES FAMILY

The forties brought huge disruption to family life and signalled the start of a social change which would alter the structure of the family for ever. With dads away at war, mums working in factories and canteens and many children evacuated, the traditional family unit was split asunder. After the war the hardships continued, many families having been left homeless and without the husbands and fathers who never came home.

Evacuation

As the 1940s dawned, Britain had already been at war with Germany for three months. September 1939 had seen one and half million children and mothers move out of cities and towns to escape the anticipated air raids. By January 1940, almost half had returned to their homes.

Gerry Maloney, from South London, was seven in 1940.

'I went away in 1939 to Hove in Sussex and I was there until just before the first raid on London. The hall in Hove was packed because there were children from seven schools in the hall and people were picking out who they wanted. Out of the entire hall there were only three of us left so two old ladies took us all in, but they bullied us terribly.

'Other kids were bullied, too, and several started walking home. My friend Dennis walked all the way from Lewes in Sussex to London! I wrote to my dad and said, "If you don't come and get me, I'm walking home." So he did and I was back in London through all the raids.'

Not everybody found the experience of evacuation so traumatic. Tom Ellis, aged ten at the start of the forties, was evacuated from Erith in Kent.

'My first evacuation was to Saltwood on the Kent coast which was a clever move on behalf of the government, considering where

---

Previous pages - Left: Families who had lost their homes in bombing raids were given temporary prefabricated houses during the post-war housing shortage. Right: Toy manufacture ceased during the war as factories were assigned to war production.
Below: Evacuees leave London by train.

the Germans were coming from! I stayed with a lovely couple and had a very happy time. I kept in touch with them until she died a few years ago.

'My sister was evacuated to Canterbury, because she was in a different school. She was five years older than me. As Hitler advanced it was realized that Kent wasn't such a good place for us to be so my school was re-evacuated to Wales. They were nice people but it was a farming community and they would lapse into Welsh and talk amongst themselves. The school itself continued to act as one school because we had our own classes, so we didn't mix. All our weekend activities were school clubs and the teachers were evacuated with us.

'I did miss my family but it was such a pleasant atmosphere and little kids don't worry very much. My mum and dad came down to see me sometimes. On one occasion, I was told I was going to get a great present at Christmas. I was convinced it was a bicycle and it turned out to be my father! I was so disappointed!'

Mothers with younger children were often evacuated with them and some were lucky enough to keep the whole family together. Kath Jarman was one of six sisters evacuated from Dockhead in South London. She and her family stayed in Hailsham, in Kent, for the duration of the war.

'My mother came with us because my youngest sister was still a baby. We stayed at the vicarage for a couple of days eating our rations of dry biscuits and chocolate. Then people came in to choose who they wanted. My mum said, 'If you take one you take them all.' So we ended up with the bottom part of a house and another family from Dockhead had the upstairs.

'My mum died two years afterwards of TB. Mary was the eldest sister but she was in the land army, although they kept her local so she could be near us, but Joan, who was thirteen

Above: Volunteers were required to help relocate children evacuated from Britain's cities.

when the war started, brought us up. My dad used to come down every weekend but we were lucky because we had each other.

'Joan went to work eventually in a rope factory. We didn't need anyone to look after us because we all looked after the younger ones as we got older. We could all

1940
8 January: Weekly food rations begin — 4 ozs for butter or lard, 12 ozs for sugar, 4 ozs for raw bacon or ham (3.5 ozs for cooked) and 2 eggs.

Above: Tearful mothers watch their children depart from London's Waterloo Station on evacuation trains.

cook a full meal and make pies by the time we were twelve.

'The local kids didn't think much of us because they thought children from London were lousy. We really didn't mix with the Hailsham kids. The Eddicotts, who lived above us, were similar ages to us and we went to school with other evacuees, so we stuck together.'

Life in the Blitz

In September 1940 the air raids on British cities were stepped up. Heavy bombing, later referred to as 'the Blitz' (from the German *Blitzkrieg*, meaning 'Lightning War') started in London, killing 430 and injuring 1,600 in the first night. The following night another 412 were killed. The bombing raids continued until May 1941 and also targeted Liverpool, Birmingham, Plymouth, Bristol, Belfast, Manchester, Glasgow, Portsmouth, Sheffield, Newcastle, Nottingham, Hull, Southampton, Coventry and Cardiff. Some 2 million homes were destroyed and 60,000 civilians killed.

Many families had 'Anderson shelters' of corrugated iron built in the garden while others slept in street shelters or in Underground stations. Later, homes were equipped with 'Morrison shelters' – large metal structures resembling dining-room tables which people could crawl underneath in an emergency – and many chose to take their chances under one of these, or under the stairs, when the sirens sounded.

Dorothy Tripp was a housewife in North London during the Blitz.

'My son Maurice was a year and two months when the war started and for the first four years of his life, he slept under the stairs which we'd had lined with corrugated iron. He had a lovely nursery but he couldn't sleep in it. We had twin beds and we brought the mattresses down and put them on the floor of the dining room so we could see him with the door open and we could hear him if he cried.

'Eventually we had a Morrison shelter. It was wrought iron and you could fit in latticed side pieces when you went in it. Most people dug down and had a shelter built in the garden when the war started but they weren't very safe. My friend's mother was killed sleeping in an Anderson shelter because she was on the top bunk and, when a bomb went off, she fell out and hit her head on the concrete floor.

Above: Amid the ruins of their bombed-out home, two women emerge from their air-raid shelter.
Left: The conflict created an army of homeless or orphaned children.

'You never knew when you were going to be bombed. I was coming down the road from the shops one day with my cousin's wife and her son and a stray plane came over, bombing. We had to lay ourselves down on the ground with our children underneath us in the road. It was terrifying.

'No matter how many air raids we got through they never became any less terrifying.

Even if they sounded a long way away, you never knew if they would come near you.'

Back in Southwark, Gerry Maloney and his dad both had lucky escapes during an air raid.

'There were two pubs near us called the Lord Clyde and the King Henry. There was a darts match going on in both, and my dad loved a game of darts, but he didn't know which one to go to. His brother Paddy was playing at the King Henry so he went round there, then he decided to go back to the Lord Clyde. After he left, a doodlebug [V1 flying bomb] demolished the Henry and his brother was killed.

'We only went down the shelter twice, for a period. That was because we were bombed out. I was reading a book one night during the Blitz

Left: Firemen battle a blaze during the London Blitz.
Below: Coventry Cathedral was destroyed during a raid on the city in November 1940.
Right: Families rescued whatever they could carry from the rubble of their homes.

and the ceiling crashed down on me but I wasn't hurt. When we moved, another bomb caused a massive great crack all the way down our house, so we had to move again. We had to live in the shelter while we waited to be rehoused. My dad didn't believe in the shelter because he was of the opinion that if the Lord wanted you He would find you, wherever you were.'

In Coventry, the cathedral was ruined and thousands were made homeless when the city was bombed in November 1940. Ray Jennings was a teenager in the city at the time.

'I remember seeing the tower of the cathedral standing alone with nothing but rubble and smoke all around it. The street next to mine was flattened and families were wandering around with crying children in their arms, clutching little bundles of possessions and wondering where they were going to live.'

As a result of the sustained bombing, 4 million homes were damaged and 500,000 were totally destroyed. When the war ended in 1945, thousands of families were left homeless. Due to a timber shortage the government fell way short of its rebuilding target of 200,000 new homes every year and many families had to live with relatives or in cramped conditions.

Kath Jarman was one of the evacuees who returned home to find it wasn't there any more.

'We stayed six years in Hailsham and when we came back to London we stayed with my Dad's three sisters because our house had been bombed. My dad was lucky because he happened to be at his sisters' house at the time.'

1940
10 May: Prime Minister Neville Chamberlain resigns and is replaced by First Lord of the Admiralty Winston Churchill.

Women at work

Before the outbreak of war it was unusual for married women to work, but with the men away, there was a severe shortage of labour. In December 1941, Parliament passed the National Service Act, calling up all unmarried women between the ages of twenty and thirty for war work. This was soon expanded to include married women, unless they were pregnant or the mothers of young babies. The women were sent to munitions and other factories, or given work as nurses, drivers and even operating anti-aircraft guns.

Women could join one of four auxiliary services, or the Women's Voluntary Service (WVS) or the Land Army, which provided farm labour.

As a young mother, Dorothy Tripp was exempt, but others joined up straight away.

'As soon as the war started my friend Peggy thought she might be called up to work in a factory so she joined the WVS and became a full-time volunteer. She was on air-raid duty. I helped with the mobile canteens.

When people who were bombed out of their homes and had slept down the shelter would come to the canteen in the morning, we would give them sandwiches and cups of tea.'

Mary Marshall, who was an evacuee in Sussex during the war, had a variety of jobs including laundry maid, milk-van driver and shop assistant in a sweet shop. But the first day of her working life, at the tender age of fifteen, didn't go well.

'I went to a local factory called Greens. They make cakes mixtures now but at that time they were busy with the war effort and were making sandbags. I only stayed one morning as the sandbags were made from used sacks and some of them still had horse manure on them. They smelt terrible! When I came home for lunch I smelt like a pig farm. My mum went mad and said I wasn't going back. The next morning she came with me to collect my half a day's wages and when she told the foreman it was too dirty, he said, "I thought, coming from London, you'd be used to working in dirty conditions." My mum was outraged and gave him a mouthful!'

Eventually Mary joined the Land Army and was put to work on a local farm.

'Mr Burton, the farmer, was very religious and didn't allow any singing while you worked. He even told me off for whistling while I washed the milk bottles. I was absolutely terrified of cows, and he knew that, but he made me stand by the gate with a stick and shoo the cows in to be milked. Luckily the cows knew where to go. If any of them had come towards me I'd have run for my life.

'When Mr Burton was driving the milk van I had to sit on a milk crate in the back with my legs dangling out of the back. On one

Left: Women aged twenty-one and over were required to register for industrial call-up.
Above right: Women train with dummy explosives at the Royal Ordnance Factory.
Right: The Women's Voluntary Service provided food for the victims of bombing raids and for emergency workers.

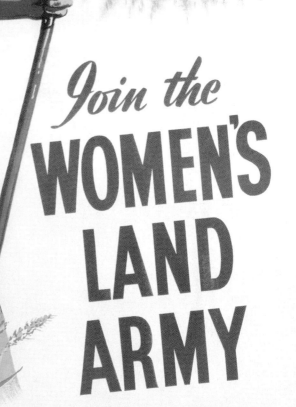

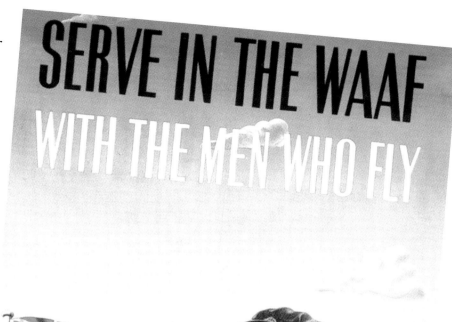

occasion we went over a bump and the milk crate slid off, with me still on it. When he realized what had happened he came back for me and had the cheek to ask me if I'd broken any bottles! I had a nasty bruise for weeks.'

Mac Black was a pupil at a boarding school in Dumfriesshire in Scotland and remembers how the war changed his mother's life.

'The war opened my mother's eyes to the fact that there was more to life than being the wife of a bank manager and a mother. She was able to become a cook at a school that had been evacuated from Suffolk to North Wales. The headmaster met her at the station and she asked him, "How many am I cooking for?" He said, "About fifty," and she said, "I've never cooked for more than four before!" He said, "Well, you can multiply, lassie, you can multiply." The next day she was cooking for fifty-odd children and the staff. My father stayed at home in Paisley but she

Left: Women were recruited to work on farms as well as in factories.
Above: Despite the government's initial reluctance to put women in uniform, their recruitment into the armed forces became inevitable.

1940
13 November: Walt Disney's musical extravaganza, *Fantasia*, premières at the Broadway Theater in New York. It is a commercial failure.

wanted to see a bit more of life and the war gave her that chance.'

By 1943 around 90 per cent of single women and 80 per cent of married women were involved in war work. After the war, the government no longer subsidized the day nurseries, so many young mothers found it impossible to carry on working. For those that did choose to stay in employment, equal pay and opportunity became a serious talking point as early as 1946. The fight for equality in the work place had begun.

The Home Guard

In May 1940, War Minister Anthony Eden broadcast a radio appeal to all able-bodied men who were not away fighting to become Local Defence Volunteers. Police stations were swamped and, by the end of June, one and half million men had been recruited. The men, later renamed the Home Guard by Winston Churchill, took over tasks such as manning anti-aircraft guns and bomb disposal, as well as nightly patrols to check that all was well in their own areas.

The public were asked to hand in their shotguns and pistols so that they could be used by the Home Guard and over 20,000 weapons were collected. The men were trained in military techniques, including sabotage and making explosive weapons to be used against an invading German army.

Ted Hughes, who was an apprentice at the Vickers-Armstrong munitions factory during the war, volunteered as a signaller in the Home Guard at Farningham, Kent. He was trained in Morse

The Local Defence Volunteers – later renamed the Home Guard – were men in reserved occupations or those too young or too old for regular military service.

code and his job was to collate the reports of local patrols.

'We were based in the billiard room of the Red Lion in Farningham. At the back of the pub was an army hut, where the others were based. The other poor so-and-sos had to go out and then report back to me. There would be me and an officer on duty all night and there was a desk, a telephone and some camp beds. There was one officer who always insisted he would go to bed properly and he used to change into his pyjamas every night.

'In our area it wasn't at all like *Dad's Army*. We were much younger because there were so many firms in the area with reserved occupations. You hear stories about the Home Guard being trained with broomsticks, and I believe that they were in some places, but Kent and Sussex were fully armed from the start, with rifles and machine guns. You were trained to use them.

'One night when I was on duty one of the first flying bombs, the V1, landed and we didn't know what it was. The patrols were saying, "I can't understand this. We saw a plane crash and we went up there, and there's just a big hole."

'If you think about it, we were the last line of resistance if the Germans had invaded. Thankfully, it didn't come to that.'

DIG FOR VICTORY

CHAPTER TWO

FOOD OF THE FORTIES

From the beginning of January 1940, throughout the decade, British families lived under rationing. The need to get by on the bare essentials dominated every aspect of life, from furniture and household goods, to cleaning materials, petrol and toys. But the family meal was the hardest hit, with enterprising housewives having to stretch meagre rations into a nutritious and filling meal for the family.

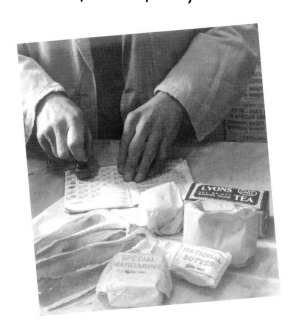

The Start of Rationing

Before the Second World War, Britain's food imports amounted to around 55 million tons a year. As an island at war, with German U-boats attacking and sinking shipping bound for Britain, such a volume of trade became impossible and food was bound to be scarce. On 8 January 1940, the inevitable rationing began, with bacon, butter and sugar the first to be restricted. Each householder was issued with a ration book and was required to register at local shops.

At that point the rations, which varied throughout the decade, were 4 ounces of butter, 12 ounces of sugar, 4 ounces of uncooked bacon or ham and 3.5 ounces of cooked bacon or ham per person, per week. Other meats were rationed a month later, followed by fish, jam, biscuits, breakfast cereals, cheese, eggs, milk and canned fruit.

Tom Ellis, who was an evacuee in Wales, remembers how food was divided up.

'The people I was with weren't in any way cruel or unfeeling but you never quite felt part of the family. You were given your pot of jam, to last a month, and your butter and cheese for the week. If you ran out, that was it. You only got one egg, but where I was, in Whitland, a lot of people kept hens to provide eggs.'

Dorothy Tripp, a housewife in North London during the forties, remembers frequent trips to the shops.

'I lived quite a walk from the shops and everything had to be carried. You'd meet someone and they'd say, "Hurry up, there's some brown bread in the baker's," or "The butcher has got some sausages" and you

---

Previous pages – Left: Government advertising campaigns encouraged self-sufficiency with neat slogans.
Right: The ration book came to dominate people's lives.

DIG FOR VICTORY LEAFLET
NUMBER 20 (NEW SERIES)

Left: Imported foods like bananas were among the first things to become unavailable.
Above: Propaganda posters and leaflets urged people to grow their own food.

dropped everything and ran straight to the shop. You had to be quick or everything would be gone.'

With food so limited, 'Dig for Victory' posters encouraged people to become more self-sufficient and grow their own vegetables, as Dorothy remembers.

'We started to grow our own potatoes and runner beans in the garden and had tomatoes in a little greenhouse. Later, we got

an allotment and grew things like carrots and parsnips which were good for stews.

'There was very little meat, particularly. There were some things they called "offal" such as liver, kidneys and sausages, which weren't rationed but they didn't last long in the shops. You had to be there the day it came in and you had to go shopping every day.

'We got one egg per person per week, so it was handy when you had a child who was too young to eat them because then you got their share! But when my son was

1941
6 February: The government publishes an official recipe for 'Blitz Broth', the first of many such 'austerity' recipes.

HUNTLEY & PALMERS BISCUITS

SUPREME IN QUALITY FOR OVER A CENTURY

DOCTOR CARROT *guards your Health*

old enough to eat eggs he was having mine as well and that's why we decided to keep six chickens in a run in our garden.

'We soon found we had more eggs than we needed and we used to sell them to some friends who had three sons. They had a ration book for each of them but growing boys eat a lot, so it wasn't very easy for them. We had to sell the eggs because it was hard getting stuff to feed the chickens. I never threw away anything like vegetable peel. I chopped it up and mixed it with corn for the chickens.'

In order to help housewives to make the best of the meagre rations, the Ministry of Food issued weekly leaflets entitled 'Food Facts'. Each offered handy hints and recipes, such as for bread without yeast, and there was general advice on how to run a household. One issue, under the heading 'Soup for Air Raids' advised: 'Try to make soup every day so you always have some ready to heat up. A hot drink works wonders at a time of shock or strain.' A recipe using standard rations

Above: Carrots were plentiful and people were urged to eat more but, while they continued to be advertised, biscuits were in short supply.

was also broadcast on the 'wireless' every morning at 8.15, and housewives became increasingly inventive in their mealtime menus.

Gillian Cook, who was living in Greenock, in Scotland, during the forties, recalls:

'I remember my mum trying to make a cake out of carrot, long before the days when carrot cake became common. It was one of the recipes issued by the Ministry of Food, because there was no candied fruit and carrots are actually quite sweet.

'You could get offal from the butcher's which was off-ration and one of the things we could get was haggis and it was just revolting. It wasn't like the haggis you get today. It was mostly oatmeal and sawdust I think, and it put me off haggis for life.'

John Wilson was a teenager in Leeds during the years of rationing.

Above: Making the most of your rations was vital to the war effort . . .
Left: . . . as was getting a good night's sleep.

'My mum used to get recipes from Marguerite Patten, who worked for the Ministry of Food and had a recipe slot on the radio. She came up with things like "Monday Pie" which was a way of using up any leftovers from a Sunday joint. Shepherd's pie wasn't only made with beef or lamb – we did it with chicken or pork. If you could get a chicken you were lucky because that didn't come under rationing and neither did rabbit, but they were quite expensive.

'We ate a lot of stews because that made the meat go further. If you saved your meat rations for a couple of weeks you could get a small joint and any leftovers were used to make stew and the bones were boiled down to make gravy or soup.'

Above: These Scouts are collecting material for recycling.
Below: Sadly, hard-working children were unlikely to get their hands on sweets like these.

Children and Rationing

As children need certain vitamins and minerals to promote growth, they were given priority in the ration programme. They received their own ration books which included special coupons for cod-liver oil and orange juice and mothers could register for a government milk scheme to obtain

Sharps
THE WORD FOR
TOFFEE

EDWARD SHARP & SONS LTD
of Maidstone, Kent
"THE TOFFEE SPECIALISTS"

"Mars ARE MARVELLOUS"

You'll certainly agree! Just taste these chunks of sheer delicious goodness made with chocolate to sustain, glucose to energise, milk to nourish you. Ask your sweet shop for Mars.

Mars

milk for children under five. In 1941, a vitamin welfare scheme was launched to combat malnourishment in youngsters, with those under two receiving free blackcurrant juice and cod-liver oil. Certain fruits, especially oranges, were hard to come by and bananas disappeared from the shops altogether.

Maurice Tripp was still a baby when rationing began.

'I remember people saying to me, "Poor little boy, he's never had a banana." I didn't even know what a banana looked like. When I finally tasted one I was so disappointed because I didn't actually like them very much!'

Famous brands of the forties included Virol malt and Ovaltine, while gravy came from Bisto and custard from Birds. Mars bars were available but, because of distribution restrictions, only to the people of Slough! Elsewhere Rowntrees provided chocolate while Bassett's Allsorts were a firm favourite in the North. But for the children growing up in the forties, sweet rationing was, perhaps, the biggest hardship of all.

Gillian Cook from Greenock remembers her weekly visit to the sweet shop.

'We got 2 ounces of sweets a week and my sister Sally and I always ate ours in one go. My mother loved Toblerone and she used to make her 2 ounces of Toblerone last all

GOOD NIGHT!

CHECKING endless bills of lading, chasing up belated consignments, answering a telephone that never stops ringing—she's doing a key job for Britain in a busy ... It's one mad rush all day long but, like so many people wh... t, she finds that a steaming goodnight cup of Bourn-vita ... her restful sleep and renewed energy—and that's what ... keep up the effort demanded of us today.

GOOD MOR...

★ CADBURY

Bourn-

For extra effort - e...

The
Cup that Cheers

DRINK a cup of 'Ovaltine' before and after a spell of duty. It will help you to keep cheerful and fit, and will maintain your strength, energy and stamina under the most arduous conditions.

'Ovaltine' is 100 per cent. health-giving, energy-building nourishment. A cupful quickly restores vitality, builds up resistance and prevents any ill-effects from exposure or fatigue.

'Ovaltine' is packed in air-tight tins and is easily prepared, with either milk or water. It can be eaten dry, if desired. Remember to order 'Ovaltine' in the canteen.

Delicious

Ovaltine

Above: Brand leaders turned patriotism into a marketing tool.

1941
7 December: A Japanese naval task force launches the infamous attack on Pearl Harbor that brings America into the war.

week. She wouldn't let us have any, which was fair enough because we ate all ours in twenty seconds. My great aunt was quite high up in the Red Cross in the west of Scotland and she would do these tours of hospitals. There was a special hospital for the soldiers from Canada and they were smashing. Because they were away from their families, they thought Sally and I were fantastic so they would ply us with sweets!'

Tom Ellis remembers trying to find other ways to satisfy his craving for sweets.

'Me and my friend Ron discovered we

A **M**essage of **C**heer . . .

Not all our trials can repress the immemorial joys of Christmas; rather, in our fortitude, will they bring us new delight.

For we have reason in plenty for thanksgiving. What means a temporary tightening of belts, a touch of what is called 'austerity,' a reshuffling of our duties, when we contemplate the might-have-been!

Good things still come to cheer our Christmas tables — McVitie & Price Biscuits happily among them.

What odds if they're a little less abundant; assuredly we shall enjoy them all the more.

M‘Vitie & Price Ltd
Biscuit Manufacturers
Edinburgh . London . Manchester

could buy sweet things in chemists – cough sweets and chewing gum – and we got hold of some laxative dates. We tried them and decided they weren't quite as nice as we'd thought and we gave them to the little boy next door, who ate the lot!'

Kath Jarman, who was evacuated to Hailsham, East Sussex, with her five sisters, admits to her own desperate measures.

'We managed on rationing but, quite honestly, we didn't have the money to buy any more than our weekly ration anyway. My spinster aunts used to come down and they never bought any sweets, but they used to take our bacon ration for themselves! I was so desperate I remember pinching a little packet of chewing gum and then being terrified after I'd left the shop.'

Cookery lessons at school presented another problem for Kath.

'My sister Joan was looking after us and I didn't ask her for food to take in because I knew it wasn't there. Instead I used to go round to my friend Rita's house and cadge from her, because her dad always had lots of fruit and veg. My dad didn't have enough money to buy things for six children.'

Christmas and Special Occasions

As the forties progressed, food became more and more scarce and Christmases were harder to cater for. The Ministry of Food leaflets suggested recipes for such treats as chocolate squares ('An extra sweet for the stocking!'), icing made without icing sugar and 'mock' cream.

Kath Jarman recalls:

'I only remember celebrating one Christmas during the war – six months after my mum died. Dad came down to see us. He tried to hitchhike but ended up walking most of the way. As soon as he got through the door he burst into tears and cried his eyes out. I wasn't expecting a present but he gave me a doll, which I loved.'

YULE
NEED

SOME OF YOUR COUPONS
for

BARKER & DOBSON'S

CHOCOLATES AND SWEETS

WHICH WILL, WE HOPE, SOON BE AVAILABLE
FOR OUR OVERSEAS FRIENDS ALSO

Barker & Dobson, Liverpool, England.

Both pages: For many manufacturers, especially at Christmas, keeping their brand names alive meant advertising goods they couldn't deliver!

In the spirit of the time, many soldiered on and improvised as well as they could when it came to Christmas Day. Dorothy Tripp remembers one special Christmas at home:

'The Morrison shelter nearly filled my dining room. We used it for Christmas one year and we had twenty to dinner! We had to bring benches home because you couldn't fit chairs around it. It wasn't easy with the rationing but we got by somehow and I did it all on our ration book.

'My dad worked for a butcher and he got me a turkey, as he did every Christmas. You didn't get much, I can tell you. I got the veg and potatoes from the allotment and garden.'

When it came to special occasions, Dorothy remembers many joint efforts.

'You couldn't make a christening cake or wedding cake on your own rations, so if there was a special occasion everybody would club together and get different things for your cake. If someone else was in need, or there was a special occasion, we happily chipped in.'

Of course, the biggest special occasion of all was VE Day (Victory in Europe), on 8 May 1945. The war in Europe had officially ended and impromptu parties sprang up all over the country, with people bringing whatever rations they could scrape together to help celebrate the historic event.

Gerry Maloney, from Dockhead, was a fifteen-year-old on VE Day.

'My friend Lennie worked as a driver for Courage Breweries and on VE Day he was driving through the West End and everybody started jumping on the back of his van and heaving crates off it. He couldn't drive away because there were so many people so he phoned the brewery and they said "Let them

Again not this Xmas.

but . . .

Yes, we know that you would love to obtain a delicious Marsh Ham this Christmas : but, until official restrictions are lifted you'll just have to wait and look forward. And, we hope you will not have to wait too long.

MARSH'S HAM

MARSH & BAXTER LTD.,
BRIERLEY HILL, STAFFS.

have it!" so he started giving it out!

'We all went berserk in the streets and had big bonfires. We burnt a big hole in the asphalt of the road. Everybody had flags out and people put stalls up in the street. It was terrific.'

After the War

The end of the war provided no respite from rationing. In fact, the food shortage was so serious that new foods had to be rationed. Potatoes, available throughout the conflict, were rationed in 1947 and bread was rationed for two years between 1946 and 1948. A new scheme, known as Bread Units (BUs) awarded a different number of weekly points to each person every week, according to age and requirement, with extra BUs being awarded to manual workers. Two BUs bought a small loaf of bread while three were needed for one pound of flour.

Many restrictions remained into the 1950s, with meat rationing the last to go in 1954. By 1948, weekly rations were 1.5 ounces of cheese, 7 ounces of butter, 8 ounces of sugar, 2 ounces of tea, 4 ounces of sweets, 3 pints of milk, 4 ounces of preserves. One person was also allowed 2 ounces of bacon and ham a fortnight and one egg per ration book, when available.

Gillian Cook remembers bread rationing all too well:

'Bread rationing was awful because my sister and I loved bread. We once ate a whole loaf before we'd got it home from the baker's, then we had to confess to my mother that we'd eaten the whole bread ration.'

Your perfect laxative

Gently and safely, without fail, Beecham's Pills will keep you really well. The blessings of cheerfulness and energy, which to a large extent depend upon your obedience to the golden rule of health, will be yours to the full if you take this famous home medicine.

Beecham's Pills

WORTH A GUINEA A BOX

Opposite: Celebrating the end of the war at a holiday camp in England, summer 1945.
Above and below: Magazine advertising for the healthy and the not-so-healthy.

1942
3 February: The government imposes clothes price restrictions, limiting the cost of a suit to £4 18s 8d (£4.93)

Magistrate : "So you broke into a grocer's shop to get a bottle of HP Sauce. Then what were you doing at the safe ? "

Prisoner : "That's where they keep it now, yer 'onor."

HP sauce

IN GREAT DEMAND BUT VERY LIMITED SUPPLY

There's nothing like a Guinness after a hard day's work · · ·

Guinness

IS GOOD FOR YOU

AFTER SIX YEARS

HENNESSY

JA. HENNESSY & C?
COGNAC

BETTER THAN EVER

Now that imported waters are no longer available— try something you will like better

Schweppes

MALVERN SPA

Order from your Wine Merchant, Grocer or Chemist.

Both pages: Shortages of all kinds continued after the war, but even when goods were available, people had to manage their incomes most carefully, as the table of average earnings shows.

but I've got a tin of NESCAFÉ

The lucky man who's got the tin of Nescafé is sure of trouble-free performance all the time. No tinkering — no bother. Just make Nescafé right in the cup, and you have perfect, full-flavoured fragrant coffee without a hitch. Demand is ever growing, and supplies do not yet keep pace with it. But you'll get your chance, and then for Nescafé. None of the drawbacks but all the enjoyment of really delicious coffee.

NESCAFÉ IS A SOLUBLE COFFEE PRODUCT composed of coffee solids, with dextrins, maltose and dextrose, added to retain the aroma.

A NESTLÉ'S PRODUCT

...K THEY COME

...E BY ONE

With beach defences removed, youth is swimming again in the silver sea round this "Sceptred Isle". Symbolic also of the joy of a peacetime setting, the '57 Varieties' with all their goodness and appetising flavour, are coming back — one by one.

HEINZ 57 VARIETIES

ALREADY ABOUT: Baked Beans, Spaghetti, Soups, Sandwich Spread, Salad Cream, Pickles and Vinegar.

AVERAGE WAGES

In the 1940s skilled and unskilled workers in the building trades were expected to work in excess of 50 hours per week. The average daily rates of pay for building workers varied across the country, but in the south of England they were:

YEAR	SKILLED		UNSKILLED	
1940	17s 6d	(87p)	13s 7d	(68p)
1941	18s 4d	(92p)	14s 5d	(72p)
1942	18s 9d	(94p)	14s 10d	(74p)
1943	19s 7d	(98p)	15s 5d	(77p)
1944	£1 0s 5d	(£1.02)	16s 1d	(80p)
1945	£1 1s 3d	(£1.06)	17s 1d	(85p)
1946	£1 4s 7d	(£1.23)	19s 10d	(99p)
1947	£1 7s 1d	(£1.35)	£1 1s 8d	(£1.08)
1948	£1 7s 6d	(£1.37)	£1 2s 1d	(£1.10)
1949	£1 7s 11d	(£1.40)	£1 2s 11d	(£1.15)

The figures in brackets are the direct modern decimal equivalents with no adjustment for inflation. The price of the *Daily Mail* newspaper shows how the buying power of the pound has changed.

In 1940 a *Daily Mail* cost one penny (1d); today it costs 40p, equivalent to 8 shillings or 96 times the 1940 price.

Commanding Attention

From her uniform a woman demands the outstanding qualities which only faultless tailoring and the finest cloth available can produce. We believe that the secret of distinction lies in attention to detail plus intelligent application of regulation requirements to individual needs. Our service extends to all feminine uniform accessories.

Telephone: Regent 6789

AUSTIN REED OF REGENT STREET AND PRINCIPAL CITIES

CHAPTER THREE

FASHIONS ON RATIONS

In the early part of the forties, for the first time ever, fashion was governed from the political chambers of Westminster rather than the fashion houses of Paris. The British population were told what they could buy, what they could wear and even how long their socks should be. It wasn't until 1947 that the 'New Look' changed women's wardrobes from the austere to the elegant.

Clothes Rationing

On 1 June 1940, clothes rationing was introduced and special clothing coupons were issued. Initially adults were allocated 66 coupons a year while the child's allocation depended on age and size. The number of coupons was later cut to 48, then 36 and eventually 20. A man's suit would need 22 coupons while a coat cost 16 and a dress 11.

Towards the end of 1941, 'Utility Clothing' was introduced in an attempt to combat the growing cost of clothes and the shortage of materials. A multitude of regulations governed the manufacture of garments, including a maximum length for skirts, a restriction on pocket size and a ban on turn-ups. Frills on underwear were banned and calf-length socks for men were replaced by ankle socks.

With so many women doing manual work, style was less important than practicality, and dungarees and trousers, worn with headscarves, became commonplace. For women working in an office rather than on the land or the factory floor, the skirts were straight and the shoes practical and comfortable.

As the materials and labour became more scarce, with vital resources devoted to the war effort, families had to get used to shortages and make do with what little they could get.

As one of six girls, Kath Jarman recalls getting by on the bare minimum.

'I remember having one pair of socks and having to wash them out, iron them dry and put them on again. One of my sisters had one dress that she wore to school every day and she would wash it out every night to wear again. When girls at school mentioned it she said "It's only my school dress. I don't wear this on a Sunday." But we accepted it and you got used to not having anything.'

Gillian Cook, growing up in Greenock, says that mothers became experts in turning something for which they had no use into something more worthwhile.

'People managed very well on clothing rations which were very tight. You couldn't get any clothing or material which was very hard if you had a big family. My mother used to make things for myself and my sister. She made me a dressing gown out of a blanket.'

Carefully composed

To give top value for your precious coupons. Perfect style with extra comfort plus. An American fashion shoe — Brannock fitted with 5 fittings to each size and half size.

Seltona

MADE BY
SEXTON OF NORWICH

Previous pages – Left: Officers who could afford individual tailoring did not have to rely on the uniform issued by their quartermaster. Right: This symbol was carried on utility clothing and even furniture manufactured to the government's specifications.

Make Do and Mend

As the clothing shortage continued, the government promoted the slogan 'Make Do and Mend'. Women were encouraged to repair what they could and make new things out of old. Women's magazines were full of tips on mending clothes and government publications included such titles as 'New Life for Old Sheets', which advised women to cut worn sheets down the middle and sew them back together, and 'Turn and Turn About', advising them to rotate sheets and blankets to save wear. One, entitled 'Patriotic Patches', advised 'A neatly patched garment is something to be proud of these days. To discard clothes that are not completely worn out is as unpatriotic as to waste good food.'

Dorothy Tripp was a dab hand with a needle and, with a husband at home and a growing child, that proved to be a blessing.

'I was fortunate because I could make things. I used to go up to Berwick market and get some lovely material for two shillings and sixpence [12.5p] a yard, and I made my own clothes. It helped a lot because I had more coupons for my son, Maurice, and my husband, Jim. Children's clothes were hard to get, and I made most of Maurice's clothes when he was very little. I would cut away the back of Jim's old shirts, which were always perfect, and

Opposite: Restrictions on clothing manufacture included limiting the height of shoe heels to two inches.
Right and below: High Street names were keen to supply the armed forces.

make them into little shirts for Maurice. His trousers I made from the bottom section of the legs of Jim's long trousers because that was never worn. I was able to save my coupons for the essentials like shoes, which were hard to get.

'When Maurice first went to school he had to wear grey trousers and white shirts, which I made, but they had to have a blazer and that was all I had to find coupons for. A lot of the kids didn't have enough coupons for everything so they had to go without a blazer.

'I made a bit of money making things for other people. I would make someone a dress for five shillings [25p], but I really didn't have a lot of time to do needlework, and I only had

Left: Women were encouraged to make repairs instead of buying new.
Below: Berkertex models pose in utility dresses by designer Norman Hartnell.
Opposite: Woman magazine advertises 'coupon-saving patterns' to make your own outfits as clothes rationing continued in 1946.

Woman

★ **SPECIAL COUPON-SAVING PATTERNS** — see

an

1942
18 February: Due to the shortage of cosmetics, women are reported to be using cooked beetroot juice for lipstick and soot for mascara.

Below left: Although ideal utility wear, this blouse and dungarees would have been unthinkable before the war.
Below right: With neither silk nor the new nylon stockings available in wartime Britain, some women resorted to having their legs dyed and stocking seams painted on.
Opposite: Practical they may have been, but these suits cost more than a week's wages for most people. Churchill was a devotee of what were known as 'siren suits', though his were mainly made by Austin Reed.

old hand sewing machine so I only did things for very close friends.'

Mary Marshall's father had his work cut out when he came to see his evacuated children in Sussex.

'Often, when my dad came for the weekend, he spent all the time mending our shoes. He would bring down a piece of leather and a foot cast and sit down to mend two or three pairs of shoes with a mouthful of nails. We were always frightened he would swallow them. Then he would melt this toffee-like substance and put it round the outside of the

What you need in an air raid

The Simpson tailored shelter suit—good looking and practical in every way. Slipped on as one garment in half a jiffy. Trousers detachable from the coat. In soft warm fleece — navy and natural. Price 70/- for men.
For women 69/6.
With a hood 82/6.

Simpson PICCADILLY

REGENT 2002

leather, which was always black or brown. Sometimes he only had black, and it was too bad if the shoes he was mending were brown. If they wore out between mending, we put cardboard in to keep the rain out.'

Hats, Bags and Stockings

There may have been a war on but British women were determined to keep up appearances.

As clothes were necessarily plain, many found ways to accessorize with style. Hats, gloves and handbags were essential details to finish off an outfit. Gas masks had to be carried at all times, so larger bags were soon in vogue, many with a false bottom to house the mask discreetly.

Hats were particularly popular as they were one of the few things that didn't require coupons. Flowers and feathers were also off the ration list, making amateur millinery all the rage. Dorothy Tripp made herself a very glamorous hat.

'I went to a jumble sale and found myself in possession of a brown woollen coat with a fur collar. So I made myself a pillbox hat and put two fur pockets at the bottom. Looking back it was a bit old for me really, but my mum said I looked lovely. The first time I wore it out, I felt a bit too made up so I took it off.'

Eventually Dorothy took a temporary job at a milliner's in North London.

'I went one day and there was a notice in the window saying "Assistant needed" so I went in. I'd never done it before but I'd always wanted to be a milliner only my dad couldn't afford it. The shop owner was pregnant and needed someone to work in the shop while she sat in the work room out the back, so I worked there until she had the baby.

'In those days it was either hats with very wide brims or no brim at all, in the pillbox

Swirla SKIRTS

Trim hip and waistline—fine fabric finely tailored— and always the joy of a graceful swing. From shops and stores at prices from 24/- to 30/-.

Write to us for your nearest stockist :—
M. & S. GREEN LTD., 12/26 Lexington Street, London, W.1

Both pages: Once manufacturing restrictions were lifted, high heels and flowing lines were the order of the day.

style. We would take a huge piece of felt and heat it up with a special electric heater then, when it was warm, we'd push it down over a mould. Then we would cut the brim and trim it with ribbons or flowers. Veils and netting were very popular but we couldn't always get the things we wanted. We could get ribbon, but you didn't get much of a choice when it came to colour. We made our own flowers for the hats but most materials were hard to get because the mills were making cloth for uniforms.'

Silk stockings were in short supply due to the textile shortages and, while nylon stockings had been produced by Du Pont in

**1943
22 September:
Plans for PAYE –
Pay As You Earn –
income tax
deductions direct
from workers'
wages are
announced.**

47

Even an archaeologist can't go on living in the Stone Age for ever. I'll excavate myself from these Roman ruins to-morrow. Can't let these young chaps get away with everything—after all some of the Greek Gods were about my own age.

POINTS TO PONDER ON

1. MOULDED TO FIT MASCULINE FIGURE.
2. Y-FRONT OPENING NEVER GAPES.
3. FITTED TO HIP MEASUREMENT.
4. SHORTS AND MIDWAYS.
5. NEED NO IRONING—NO BUTTONS TO COME OFF.
6. FROM 4/5 EACH.

★ Normally obtainable at leading Men's Shops

Coopers Y-front UNDERWEAR

LYLE & SCOTT LTD., ARGYLL STREET, LONDON. W.I. AND HAWICK, SCOTLAND

what is Lastex?

※ Lastex is the miracle elastic yarn that gives invisible and lasting elasticity to your clothes. Woven into corsets, frocks, lingerie, swimsuits, it keeps them snug and sleek. It's slenderising and supremely comfortable. Look for the Lastex Label—the sign of figure-caressing stretch that defies wear and washing.

LASTEX YARN & LACTRON THREAD LTD. (Dept. W), St. Mary's Mills, LEICESTER.
47L/10

Sirdar Leaflet No. 1192.

Lady's Jumper with striped yoke (bust 35 inches) in Sirdar Majestic Wool 3-ply. Sirdar Wools obtainable from retailers only, leaflets from retailers price 4d., or post free 5d., from Dept. A :—

HARRAP BROS. (SIRDAR WOOLS) LTD., BECTIVE MILLS, WAKEFIELD

the USA since 1938, they were largely unavailable in Britain before 1948, when they began to be manufactured on a large scale in Pontypool. One or two girls managed to get hold of these precious accessories by fraternizing with the American soldiers stationed in the UK, but for the rest of the female population it was time to improvise.

Shops began to offer stocking-darning services but many girls used leg make-up with an eyebrow-pencil 'seam' line drawn up the back. Those who couldn't afford the make-up used gravy browning – and prayed it wouldn't rain!

Mary Marshall remembers helping out an employer with fake stockings.

'When I worked in a sweet shop the owner, Eileen, had legs like bottles and had rather thick hair all over them. She asked me to paint on some liquid stockings, from a bottle, as she couldn't get any stockings. I couldn't bring myself to touch her legs so I did it with cotton wool.'

The New Look

Although clothes were still rationed after the war, the mood of celebration meant that many were ready for something new in the wardrobe. In 1947 French designer Christian Dior introduced his 'New Look'. The square-shouldered jacket and short skirt were replaced with flattering bust-lines, a tight-fitting waist and full, billowing skirts that reached the calves. High heels were also back in fashion.

Princess Margaret was one of the first in Britain to adopt the New Look, and many others followed.

Julia Temple was a teenager in Newcastle at the time.

'After the plain, practical clothes of the war years, with the clumpy shoes, we were really excited when we saw the pictures of the lovely new designs. We thought Princess Margaret was the height of glamour and I was really jealous when a girl in our road had the first "New Look" outfit. It made all our clothes look really dull.'

Other influences came from America, with the film stars of the day leading the trends, as Kath Jarman remembers:

'I made most of my own clothes and I used to wear the dirndl skirts, gathered at the waist. I used to think I looked like Doris Day. The dresses were always flowing, not straight. I saw a film with her which had a navy and white dress with a bow and I went out and bought one that was nearly identical, and I thought I looked great.'

Women weren't the only ones to be influenced by the fashion of the films. The gangster movies coming over from America led to boys getting in on the fashion trends, as Gerry Maloney remembers:

'All the lads were getting made-to-measure

Both pages: New Look skirts were extravagantly flared, and there were new things going on underneath, too.

suits. They were twenty coupons and nobody had enough, but you could go into a tailor's shop and pay a little extra money and you didn't need so many coupons. I had my first made-to-measure suit made at fourteen at a place called Nathan's. It was brilliant. It was the only brown suit I've ever had. It was "full drape", which meant that if you put your arms down beside you the sleeves had to come down to the fingertips. You could have them single or double breasted but the shoulders were huge, with a ton of padding. The trousers were about 18- or 19-inch bottom but it didn't matter much as long as the jacket was right.

'Very few of us had belts. It had to be

THE FORTIES
Good Times Just Around The Corner

Both pages: The elegance of the post-war designs contrasts starkly with the wartime pattern booklet for 'Make-do and Mend' slippers.

braces to make the trousers hang straighter. They were smarter, unless you took your jacket off but nobody ever did. We never went casual, even when we were out for a drink. We would even sit on a beach with a suit on!'

1944
6 June: In the biggest combined air and sea assault ever staged, Allied troops storm the Normandy beaches on D-Day.

THE MOVIES OF THE FORTIES

Going to the cinema was the highlight of the week for millions during the forties, where people not only saw hugely popular movies like *Sinbad the Sailor*, but also caught up with current events, watching newsreels much as we tune in to the television news. During the war, established movie stars played patriotic roles in films that fused entertainment with propaganda, but some, like Major David Niven, Colonel James Stewart and Captain Clark Gable (opposite) were determined to do their duty in uniform and joined the armed forces.

OSCARS 1940

BEST ACTOR	James Stewart — *The Philadelphia Story*
BEST SUPPORTING ACTOR	Walter Brennan — *The Westerner*
BEST ACTRESS	Ginger Rogers — *Kitty Foyle*
BEST SUPPORTING ACTRESS	Jane Darwell — *The Grapes of Wrath*
BEST SONG	'When You Wish Upon A Star' from *Pinocchio*
BEST MOVIE	*Rebecca* — Selznick International Pictures

OSCARS 1941

BEST ACTOR	Gary Cooper — *Sergeant York*
BEST SUPPORTING ACTOR	Donald Crisp — *How Green Was My Valley*
BEST ACTRESS	Joan Fontaine — *Suspicion*
BEST SUPPORTING ACTRESS	Mary Astor — *The Great Lie*
BEST SONG	'The Last Time I Saw Paris' from *Lady Be Good*
BEST MOVIE	*How Green Was My Valley* — 20th Century-Fox

OSCARS 1942

BEST ACTOR	James Cagney — *Yankee Doodle Dandy*
BEST SUPPORTING ACTOR	Van Heflin — *Johnny Eager*
BEST ACTRESS	Greer Garson — *Mrs Miniver*
BEST SUPPORTING ACTRESS	Teresa Wright — *Mrs Miniver*
BEST SONG	'White Christmas' from *Holiday Inn*
BEST MOVIE	*Mrs Miniver* — Metro-Goldwyn-Mayer

OSCARS 1943

BEST ACTOR	Paul Lukas — *Watch on the Rhine*
BEST SUPPORTING ACTOR	Charles Coburn — *The More the Merrier*
BEST ACTRESS	Jennifer Jones — *The Song of Bernadette*
BEST SUPPORTING ACTRESS	Katina Paxinou — *For Whom the Bell Tolls*
BEST SONG	'You'll Never Know' from *Hello, Frisco, Hello*
BEST MOVIE	*Casablanca* — Warner Bros

OSCARS 1944

Best Actor	Bing Crosby — *Going My Way*
Best Supporting Actor	Barry Fitzgerald — *Going My Way*
Best Actress	Ingrid Bergman — *Gaslight*
Best Supporting Actress	Ethel Barrymore — *None but the Lonely Heart*
Best Song	'Swinging on a Star' *from Going My Way*
Best Movie	*Going My Way* — Paramount

OSCARS 1945

Best Actor	Ray Milland — *The Lost Weekend*
Best Supporting Actor	James Dunn — *A Tree Grows in Brooklyn*
Best Actress	Joan Crawford — *Mildred Pierce*
Best Supporting Actress	Anne Revere — *National Velvet*
Best Song	'It Might As Well Be Spring' from *State Fair*
Best Movie	*The Lost Weekend* — Paramount

OSCARS 1946

BEST ACTOR	Fredric March — *The Best Years of Our Lives*
BEST SUPPORTING ACTOR	Harold Russell — *The Best Years of Our Lives*
BEST ACTRESS	Olivia de Havilland — *To Each His Own*
BEST SUPPORTING ACTRESS	Anne Baxter — *The Razor's Edge*
BEST SONG	'On the Atchison, Topeka and the Santa Fe' from *The Harvey Girls*
BEST MOVIE	*The Best Years of Our Lives* — Samuel Goldwyn Productions

OSCARS 1947

BEST ACTOR	Ronald Colman — *A Double Life*
BEST SUPPORTING ACTOR	Edmund Gwenn — *Miracle on 34th Street*
BEST ACTRESS	Loretta Young — *The Farmer's Daughter*
BEST SUPPORTING ACTRESS	Celeste Holm — *Gentleman's Agreement*
BEST SONG	'Zip-A-Dee-Doo-Dah' from *Song of the South*
BEST MOVIE	*Gentleman's Agreement* — 20th Century-Fox

OSCARS 1948

BEST ACTOR	Laurence Olivier — *Hamlet*
BEST SUPPORTING ACTOR	Walter Huston — *The Treasure of the Sierra Madre*
BEST ACTRESS	Jane Wyman — *Johnny Belinda*
BEST SUPPORTING ACTRESS	Claire Trevor — *Key Largo*
BEST SONG	'Buttons and Bows' from *The Paleface*
BEST MOVIE	*Hamlet* — J. Arthur Rank-Two Cities Films

OSCARS 1949

BEST ACTOR	Broderick Crawford — *All the King's Men*
BEST SUPPORTING ACTOR	Dean Jagger — *Twelve O'Clock High*
BEST ACTRESS	Olivia de Havilland — *The Heiress*
BEST SUPPORTING ACTRESS	Mercedes McCambridge — *All the King's Men*
BEST SONG	'Baby, It's Cold Outside' from *Neptune's Daughter*
BEST MOVIE	*All the King's Men* — Robert Rossen Productions

Left: In the 1946 tearjerker The Yearling, *Claude Jarman Jnr played a boy who adopts a young deer, with Gregory Peck and Jane Wyman as his parents.*
Right: Bing Crosby won the 1944 Best Actor Oscar in the movie Going My Way.

CHAPTER FOUR

STAYING IN

Home life in the forties revolved around the family, and evenings were often spent around the fire chatting, reading or listening to the radio. In the absence of television, and with newspapers reduced to four pages, radio was the main source of information and entertainment. Mealtimes were usually spent eating together, around a table, and parties at home were a popular way to socialize with friends and neighbours.

Radio

The radio was hugely important in the majority of British homes throughout the forties. It provided listeners with information on rationing, recipes and tips, and supplied news about the progress of Allied forces abroad, although the latter was strictly censored so as not to reveal too much to the enemy. It also provided light entertainment, music and sports news.

Previous pages – Left: Muffin the Mule became a firm TV favourite with children from his very first appearance on the BBC in 1946.

Above: The Radio Fun Annual from 1943 featured Arthur Askey introducing a host of caricatured radio favourites.

Opposite: Every home had to have a radio, no matter what the price.

At the start of the war the BBC replaced its National and Regional programmes with 'The Home Service', which was initially criticized by listeners for having too many organ recitals and public announcements. The BBC's response was to create the weekly comedy show *ITMA*, which stood for *It's That Man Again* and was named after a phrase that newspapers commonly used when referring to Hitler. Liverpudlian comedian Tommy Handley was the front man and, with the help of Ted Kavanagh, he created one of the most popular shows of the era.

Other much-loved programmes during the war included *The Brains Trust, Desert Island Discs* and *Workers' Playtime,* while the late forties brought *Mrs Dale's Diary, Housewives' Choice* and *Dick Barton Special Agent.*

Favourite comedians included Max Miller, Arthur Askey and Tommy Trinder. Children had their own treat with *Children's Hour* presented by 'Uncle Mac', otherwise known as Derek McCulloch.

Ted Hughes spent many an evening at home, with wife Maisie, listening to the radio.

'I loved *Round the Horne, ITMA* and Arthur Askey. They were silly, but it was very funny. My hobby at the time was building amplifiers, so I would be doing that and Maisie would be knitting as we listened. That's the difference between television and radio. At least you used to get things done, which you don't these days.'

Dick Barton Special Agent was a firm favourite with adults and children alike. Millions of listeners tuned in to hear the daily adventures of Dick (played by Noel Johnson), Jock and Snowy. Mac Black, who was at boarding school, was one of the many who couldn't be without his daily dose.

'If you made the mistake of being late going into one of the rooms with a radio, and you made a noise, you were in trouble. If you missed a bit of it you would be really upset.

'I listened to *ITMA,* as well, and all the

A Luxury Set
at a modest price

If you want real lifelike reproduction, a wide range of stations, and a set equipped with its own efficient built-in aerials — at a remarkably modest price — here is the set for you. Model 48A is a thorough engineering job throughout and includes such features as Pye Flywheel Tuning, Pye Tonemaster, and Extension Loud-speaker Sockets. The cabinet is beautifully finished in rich sapele mahogany. For performance, appearance and honest-to-goodness value, we are convinced that there is nothing to beat it in British Radio today. Ask your Pye Agent for further details or write to us direct.

MODEL 48A
3-waveband, mains, superhet

£25 . 9 . 9
Including Purchase Tax

MADE IN
CAMBRIDGE

King's College Chapel

1945
8 May: Following the signing of the German surrender documents, VE – Victory in Europe – Day is declared.

PYE LIMITED · RADIO WORKS · CA

Above: Tommy Handley, with script in hand, and some of his ITMA gang – Tony Francis, Derek Guyler and Molly Weir. Opposite: 'Forces Sweetheart' Vera Lynn reached into the homes of millions via the 'wireless'.

comedy programmes, but it was Dick Barton that was an absolute must. Whenever it was due to come on, we would race to find a radio.'

Music

In the late 1930s Benny Goodman formed a band and 'swing' music was born in the USA. In the early 1940s, the 'big band' sound was hugely popular in Britain, with artists like Glenn Miller, Count Basie and Dizzy Gillespie topping the popularity polls. At the same time popular music was beginning to focus on the vocalist, with singers like Frank Sinatra, the Andrew Sisters and Bing Crosby, as well as home-grown talents Anne Shelton, Gracie Fields and Vera Lynn.

In 1940, Vera Lynn's first radio programme *Sincerely Yours* was broadcast. It was a big hit with the listeners, although not with the BBC Board of Governors who dismissed its success with the comment: 'Popularity noted, but deplored'. Nevertheless, Vera Lynn's morale-boosting efforts won her the title of 'Forces Sweetheart'.

Many only heard music on the radio or at dances but, for the more fortunate, there were also gramophones and 78-rpm records. Gerry Maloney was one of the lucky ones.

AUF WIEDERSEH'N SWEETHEART

Music by EBERHARD STORCH   Words by JOHN SEXTON & JOHN TURNER

Broadcast & Recorded
ON DECCA RECORD N° F.9927
by VERA LYNN

1/-

Above: Prior to the gradual introduction of the 45-rpm disc in the 1950s, records came in a larger, 78-rpm format.
Opposite: This 1940s advertisement shows the latest television receiver from GEC.

'My mum bought me a radiogram in the late forties. You stacked ten records on it and they would crash down on top of each other and skid on each other as they span round. I listened to the Ted Heath band, Buddy de Franco, George Shearing, Al Jolson. He was going to come over here in 1950, but he died before he came. I love Frank Sinatra now, but I wasn't keen when I first heard him. I thought he was a bit pathetic. I thought Crosby was in

a different league.'

Tom Ellis felt much the same about Ol' Blue Eyes.

'I don't think music impinged much during the war, but afterwards it was swing and big bands. Sinatra was around, but I didn't think much of him. I thought he was a bit of a weed.

Above: A family gathers round the television waiting for the evening's broadcasts to start in 1948.
Opposite: The marriage of Princess Elizabeth to Prince Philip of Greece was one of the first major events to be broadcast on British television.

I had my grandmother's gramophone, but I never bought any records for it!'

Gill Cook remembers her parents' record collection.

'My grandfather gave us a great big cabinet system with a gramophone and a radio in it, which eventually caught fire. My parents had a huge record collection of Jack Buchanan, Charlie Coombs and Noël Coward and some novelty comedy records like "Tilly took a tramp in the woods", which I eventually ended up shooting at in the garden with my air rifle because I couldn't stand it.'

Television

Although British television broadcasts had begun in the 1930s, TV was shut down for the duration of the war. In fact, so few people owned television sets that the shut-down meant very little to the average household. The BBC resumed its broadcasts on 7 June 1946 with just three and a half hours a day, and issued a £2 combined radio and TV licence. Initially, the signal could only reach those within a 30-mile radius of London, so it's not surprising that only 14,000 licences were held in 1947. But coverage and popularity were growing and by the end of 1948 the number of licence-holders had reached 150,000.

Most of the broadcasts were newsreels or special events, such as the Last Night of the Proms and the coverage of Princess Elizabeth's marriage to the Duke of Edinburgh in 1947. But younger listeners were given a special treat with *For the Children* and, from 20 October 1946, the now legendary *Muffin the Mule*.

Opposite: Frank Sinatra broke away from being merely a 'big band' singer and established himself as a solo star in the 1940s.
Above: During the war, these firemen in Croydon made toys to be sent to children's nurseries.

Ted Hughes couldn't afford a television himself, but was an occasional viewer.

'A friend of mine had a television and I would go round and watch it sometimes. You all sat round this little tiny screen, nine inches square. Everything was black and this horrible sort of blue colour. When tennis was on you had to guess where the ball was because you couldn't see it.'

Gerry Maloney caught a glimpse of a television set while away at a boys' camp.

'We went to this Major Flynn's house, which was like a castle. He had this TV which was a big thing, like a console. We were fascinated because we'd never seen anything like it. We were lucky to have a radio.'

In July 1949 the first TV weather forecast was broadcast. However, it would not be until the fifties that a television set would be less than a novelty in the British living room.

1945
6 August: The first atomic bomb is dropped on the Japanese city of Hiroshima; another will hit Nagasaki three days later.

THE FORTIES
Good Times Just Around The Corner

Toys and Games

Like everything else in the forties, material shortages meant a lack of toys. Those that were available were far too expensive for poorer families to buy: in December 1941, the smallest teddy in Hamley's retailed at 15s 6d (77p), which was a lot of money. Christmas presents, wrapped in newspaper as no wrapping paper was available, consisted of annuals, second-hand books or things that could be made by hand, like knitted dolls, gloves and slippers.

Dorothy Tripp remembers trying to find a present for her son Maurice.

'There was never anything to buy for the children. Maurice used to like the boys' annuals, so if I heard there were any at the shops just before Christmas, I'd rush and buy them. If I was lucky I got there before they were all gone.'

For children from wealthier families the more popular toys were cars, Dinky Toys and Hornby train sets. After the war plastic dolls became available and mechanical toys began to make a

comeback, with clockwork toys a favourite, if you could get to the shops before they sold out. Tricycles and bicycles were scarce and highly prized, but model kits were popular with boys.

Gerry Maloney remembers one special toy.

'My aunts lived with us and I was an only child so I got a few toys. I remember this beautiful remote-controlled car that I was given during the war. It was a magnificent red car and you plugged a wire in the back and steered it with a tiny steering wheel which sat in your hand. It must have cost a fortune.'

Maurice Tripp was a toddler when the war started.

'I can't remember any particular toys in the early years of the war, except for one wonderful box of bricks. I don't know what they were made of but they were very, very heavy and felt like stone. They were coloured and I'm sure they were German. They came in a big wooden box and you could make the most fantastic things out of them. They were very smooth.

THE FORTIES
Good Times Just Around The Corner

'Later I had the Hornby OO set, which were lovely trains. Because my father employed carpenters he had a pull-down ladder up into the loft, and he had the whole room boarded out as a playroom for me and I had a train set that went all the way round the attic.'

Gill Cook, who was growing up in Greenock and Paisley in the forties, had a great uncle with a very modern outlook on the battle of the sexes.

'Although we were girls, my great uncle was very good at buying toys and he bought us Meccano and a garage, and because it was a very big house with a huge playroom and garden, we had a great big real rocking horse. We really had the lot. You couldn't actually go out and buy toys, but I had a really rich great-aunt, Auntie Jinty, who went and bought us the most perfect coffee set, which would probably be worth a fortune now, and this was our dolls' tea set. It was an adult bone-china coffee service!'

Towards the end of the decade toys began to be manufactured in the UK on a larger scale and the shelves of the toy shops began to fill up again. In 1949, a set of wooden puppets, which were the characters for a play and could be made to dance to music, was one of the most popular toys on the market.

With new toys came new materials, with the results that synthetics and plastic became commonplace. As the decade came to a close, Ted Hughes was the proud father of his first baby daughter.

'They brought out a doll which had a synthetic covering which was just like skin. We scrimped and scraped to buy this blooming doll, which was really expensive. We bought it and she played with the box and ignored the doll!'

Which just goes to show that some things never change.

Opposite: Toys were in short supply during the war years, but by the time this picture was taken in 1949, toyshop shelves were full again. Left: These Czech toys were flown in to Northolt Aerodrome in December 1946 to be given to children in Dr Barnardo's Homes.

HITS OF THE FORTIES

There was no official 'Hit Parade' in the UK during the 1940s, the first hit singles chart not appearing until 1952, but there was a 'Hit Parade' in America and most of the American hits were also very popular in Britain. The lists of hit songs throughout this book do not, therefore, include British favourites like 'Run Rabbit Run' or 'We'll Meet Again', but are a good reflection of the music people listened and danced to in the 1940s.

TEN TOP HITS FROM 1940

I'LL NEVER SMILE AGAIN
Ruth Lowe

THE WOODPECKER SONG
Lyrics: Harold Adamson; Music: Eldo di Lazzaro

ONLY FOREVER
Lyrics: Johnny Burke; Music: James V. Monaco
From the Bing Crosby movie *Rhythm On The River*

PRACTICE MAKES PERFECT
Ernest Gold

SIERRA SUE
Joseph B. Carey
From the movie *Sierra Sue*

TRADE WINDS
Cliff Friend and Charles Tobias

WHEN YOU WISH UPON A STAR
Lyrics: Ned Washington; Music: Leigh Harline
From the movie *Pinocchio*

FRENESI
Lyrics: Ray Charles, Sidney Keith (Bob) Russell;
Music: Albert Dominguez

THERE I GO
Lyrics: Hy Zaret; Music: Irving Weiser

BLUEBERRY HILL
Al Lewis, Larry Stock and Vincent Rose
From the movie *Singing Hill*

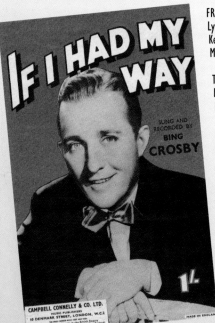

TEN TOP HITS FROM 1941

I HEAR A RHAPSODY
George Fragos, Dick Gasparre and Jack Baker

INTERMEZZO
Lyrics: Robert Henning; Music: Heinz Provost
From the movie *Intermezzo*

CHATTANOOGA CHOO CHOO
Lyrics: Mack Gordon; Music: Harry Warren

YOU AND I
Meredith Willson

AMAPOLA
Lyrics: Albert Gamse; Music: Joseph M. LaCalle

MARIE ELENA
Lyrics: Sidney Keith (Bob) Russell; Music: Lorenzo Barcelata

DADDY
Bobby Troup
From the movie *Two Latins from Manhattan*

WHITE CLIFFS OF DOVER
Lyrics: Nat Burton; Music: Walter Kent

I DON'T WANT TO SET THE WORLD ON FIRE
Bennie Benjamin, Sol Marcus, Eddie Durham and Edward Seiler

TONIGHT WE LOVE
Lyrics: Bobby Worth; Music: Freddy Martin, Ray Austin

TEN TOP HITS FROM 1942

WHITE CHRISTMAS
Irving Berlin
From the Bing Crosby movie *Holiday Inn*

HE WEARS A PAIR OF SILVER WINGS
Eric Maschwitz and Michael Carr

THERE ARE SUCH THINGS
Lyrics: Abel Baer and Stanley Adams; Music: George W. Meyer

DEEP IN THE HEART OF TEXAS
Lyrics: June Hershey; Music: Don Swander

MY DEVOTION
Roc Hillman and Johnny Nafton

I'VE GOT A GAL IN KALAMAZOO
Lyrics: Mack Gordon; Music: Harry Warren

JINGLE, JANGLE, JINGLE
Lyrics: Frank Loesser; Music: Joseph J. Lilley
From the movie *Forest Rangers*

DON'T SIT UNDER THE APPLE TREE
Lyrics: Lew Brown and Charles Tobias; Music: Sam Stept
From the stage show *Yokel Boy*

ONE DOZEN ROSES
Lyrics: Roger Lewis, Country Washburn;
Music: Dick Jurgens, Walter Donavan

SLEEPY LAGOON
Lyrics: Jack Lawrence; Music: Eric Coates

TEN TOP HITS FROM 1943

YOU'LL NEVER KNOW
Lyrics: Mack Gordon; Music: Harry Warren
From the movie *Hello, Frisco, Hello*

COMIN' IN ON A WING AND A PRAYER
Lyrics: Harold Adamson; Music: Jimmy McHugh

PAPER DOLL
Johnny S. Black
From the movie *Hi Good Lookin'*

PEOPLE WILL SAY WE'RE IN LOVE
Lyrics: Oscar Hammerstein II; Music: Richard Rodgers
From the stage show *Oklahoma!*

MY HEART TELLS ME
Lyrics: Mack Gordon; Music: Harry Warren
From the movie *Sweet Rosie O'Grady*

AS TIME GOES BY
Herman Hupfield
From the stage show *Everybody's Welcome*

SUNDAY, MONDAY, OR ALWAYS
Lyrics: Johnny Burke; Music: James Van Heusen
From the movie *Dixie*

DON'T GET AROUND MUCH ANY MORE
Lyrics: Sidney Keith (Bob) Russell; Music: Duke Ellington

MOONLIGHT BECOMES YOU
Lyrics: Johnny Burke;
Music: James Van Heusen
From the movie *Road to Morocco*

SHOO SHOO, BABY
Phil Moore

TEN TOP HITS FROM 1944

I'LL BE SEEING YOU
Lyrics: Irving Kahal;
Music: Sammy Fain
From the stage show *Right This Way*

LONG AGO AND FAR AWAY
Lyrics: Leo Robin; Music: Jerome Kern
From the movie *Cover Girl*

BESAME MUCHO
Lyrics: Sunny Skylar; Music: Consuelo Velazquez
From the movie *Follow the Boys*

I'LL WALK ALONE
Lyrics: Sammy Cahn; Music: Jule Styne
From the movie *Follow the Boys*

DON'T FENCE ME IN
Cole Porter
From the movie *Hollywood Canteen*

MAIRZY DOATS
Jerry Livingston, Al Hoffman and Milton Drake

DANCE WITH A DOLLY
Jimmy Eaton, Terry Shand and Mickey Leader

I LOVE YOU
Cole Porter
From the stage show *Mexican Hayride*

THE TROLLEY SONG
Ralph Blane and Hugh Martin
From the movie *Meet Me in St Louis*

AMOR
Lyrics: Sunny Skylar; Music: Gabriel Ruiz
From the movie *Broadway Rhythm*

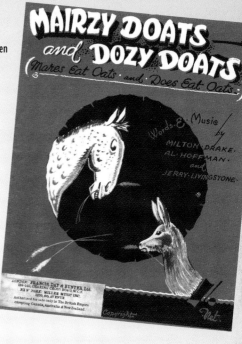

TEN TOP HITS FROM 1945

SYMPHONY
Lyrics: Jack Lawrence; Music: Alex Alstone

MY DREAMS ARE GETTING BETTER
Lyrics: Mann Curtis; Music: Vic Mizzy
From the movie *In Society*

DREAM
Johnny Mercer
From the movie *Her Highness and the Bellboy*

ACCENTUATE THE POSITIVE
Lyrics: Johnny Mercer; Music: Harold Arlen
From the movie *Here Come the Waves*

SENTIMENTAL JOURNEY
Les Brown, Ben Homer and Bud Green

IT MIGHT AS WELL BE SPRING
Lyrics: Oscar Hammerstein II; Music: Richard Rodgers
From the movie *State Fair*

IF I LOVED YOU
Lyrics: Oscar Hammerstein II; Music: Richard Rodgers
From the stage show *Carousel*

IT'S BEEN A LONG, LONG TIME
Lyrics: Sammy Cahn; Music: Jule Styne

TILL THE END OF TIME
Lyrics: Buddy Kaye; Music: Ted Mossman

I CAN'T BEGIN TO TELL YOU
Lyrics: Mack Gordon; Music: James V. Monaco
From the movie *Dolly Sisters*

TEN TOP HITS FROM 1946

THE GYPSY
Billy Reid

OH! WHAT IT SEEMED TO BE
Bennie Benjamin, George David Weiss and Frankie Carle

THEY SAY IT'S WONDERFUL
Irving Berlin
From the stage show *Annie, Get Your Gun*

TO EACH HIS OWN
Jay Livingston and Ray Evans
From the movie *To Each His Own*

LAUGHING ON THE OUTSIDE
Lyrics: Ben Raleigh; Music: Bernie Wayne

FIVE MINUTES MORE
Lyrics: Sammy Cahn; Music: Jule Styne
From the movie *Sweetheart of Sigma Chi*

A GAL IN CALICO
Lyrics: Leo Robin; Music: Arthur Schwartz
From the movie *Time, Place and The Girl*

ALL THROUGH THE DAY
Lyrics: Oscar Hammerstein II; Music: Jerome Kern
From the movie *Centennial Summer*

LET IT SNOW, LET IT SNOW, LET IT SNOW
Lyrics: Sammy Cahn; Music: Jule Styne

FOR SENTIMENTAL REASONS
Lyrics: Deke Watson; Music: William Best

TEN TOP HITS FROM 1947

OLD BUTTERMILK SKY
Hoagy Carmichael and Jack Brooks
From the movie *Canyon Passage*

PEG O' MY HEART
Lyrics: Alfred Bryan; Music: Fred Fisher
From the stage show *Ziegfeld Follies*

YOU DO
Lyrics: Mack Gordon; Music: Josef Myrow
From the movie *Mother Wore Tights*

LINDA
Lyrics: Jack Lawrence; Music: Ann Ronell
From the movie Story of *G. I. Joe*

I WISH I DIDN'T LOVE YOU SO
Frank Loesser
From the movie *Perils of Pauline*

I WONDER, I WONDER, I WONDER
Daryl Hutchins

I WONDER WHO'S KISSING HER NOW
Lyrics: Will Hough, Frank Adams;
Music: Joseph E. Howard, Harold Orlob

THAT'S MY DESIRE
Lyrics: Carroll Loveday; Music: Helmy Kresa

MAM'SELLE
Lyrics: Mack Gordon; Music: Edmund Goulding
From the movie *Razor's Edge*

ANNIVERSARY SONG
Saul Chaplin and Al Jolson

TEN TOP HITS FROM 1948

BUTTONS AND BOWS
Jay Livingston and Ray Evans
From the movie *Paleface*

A LITTLE BIRD TOLD ME
Harvey O. Brooks

ON A SLOW BOAT TO CHINA
Frank Loesser
From the movie *Neptune's Daughter*

NOW IS THE HOUR
Maewa Kaihan, Clement Scott and Dorothy Stewart

IT'S MAGIC
Lyrics: Sammy Cahn; Music: Jule Styne
From the movie *Romance on the High Seas*

**I'M LOOKING OVER A FOUR
LEAF CLOVER**
Lyrics: Mort Dixon;
Music: Harry M. Woods

YOU CALL EVERYBODY DARLING
Sam Martin, Ben L. Trace, Clem
Watts (Albert J. Trace)

**MAÑANA (IS SOON ENOUGH
FOR ME)**
Peggy Lee (had big hit recording
with hubby Dave Barbour)
From the movie *Dancing On A
Dime*

YOU CAN'T BE TRUE, DEAR
Lyrics: Hal Cotton; Music: Ken Griffen

A TREE IN THE MEADOW
Billy Reid

TEN TOP HITS FROM 1949

SOME ENCHANTED EVENING
Lyrics: Oscar Hammerstein II; Music: Richard Rodgers
From the stage show *South Pacific*

RUDOLPH THE RED-NOSED REINDEER
Johnny Marks

I CAN, DREAM CAN'T I?
Lyrics: Irving Kahal; Music: Sammy Fain
From the stage show *Right This Way*

AGAIN
Lyrics: Dorcas Cochran; Music: Lionel Newman
From the movie *Road House*

FAR AWAY PLACES
Joan Whitney and Alex Kramer

GHOST RIDERS IN THE SKY
Stan Jones
From the movie *Riders in the Sky*

POWDER YOUR FACE WITH SUNSHINE
Lyrics: Stanley Rochinski; Music: Carmen Lomnbardo

DEAR HEARTS AND GENTLE PEOPLE
Lyrics: Bob Hilliard; Music: Sammy Fain

YOU'RE BREAKING MY HEART
Pat Genaro and Sunny Skylar

CRUISING DOWN THE RIVER
Nell Tollerton and Eily Beadell

THEATRE ROYAL
LEEDS

" FAMOUS FOR PANTOMIME "

FRANCIS LAIDLER'S
Entirely New and Original Comedy Pantomime
RED RIDING HOOD

A Carnival of Fun

1. MARGERY MANNERS
2. The JOHN TILLER GIRLS
4. LILI GARDELLE
5. NORMAN EVANS

6. PERCY GARSIDE
7. BILLY PURVIS
8. The LITTLE SUNBEAMS
9. GRAY, AUSTIN AND WORTH

PROGRAMME

CHAPTER FIVE

GOING OUT

The vast majority of households were without television until the 1950s, so other forms of entertainment were both necessary and hugely popular. During the war, entertainment was an important part of maintaining morale. The Entertainments National Service Association (ENSA) was initially formed to entertain the troops and 80 per cent of British entertainers signed up. As well as performing for the armed forces, they put on shows for anyone engaged in war work, including factory staff who would have a weekly show in the canteen. Some of the shows were so bad that comedian Tommy Trinder joked that ENSA stood for 'Every Night Something Awful'. Even so, some famous names, including Tony Hancock and Gracie Fields, began their careers in ENSA.

THE FORTIES
Good Times Just Around The Corner

Dances

For most people, living conditions at home were cramped and going out seemed the obvious thing to do, although a tight budget and the strict rationing of petrol had to be taken into account. The fuel shortage and, in the early part of the decade, the war meant that most activities were local and cheap.

As an inexpensive and accessible form of entertainment dances became enormously popular. Usually held in drill halls or church halls, they were a chance for young men and women to mix with the opposite sex and meet new people. As many of the out-of-school activities were

---

Previous pages – Theatres and cinemas were initially closed down during the war, but soon re-opened for morale-boosting traditional fare.

segregated, this was an exciting prospect!

Mary Marshall looked forward to the local dances at Polegate, in Sussex.

'My friend Iris got me interested in dancing and we used to go about three times a week. It was a bit difficult when my sister started going because we were looking after the younger ones at home so we couldn't both be out at the same time. She used to go for the first half and then I would go out when she came home, but if Dad was there for the weekend we could both go. We often walked all the way home – about three miles – in the blackout. Some nights it was so dark you couldn't see a hand in front of your face, but we felt quite safe.

'One night I was at a dance at the drill hall and a Canadian soldier asked me to dance.

Both pages: Dances were an enormously popular form of entertainment, especially when the American GIs arrived to spread the 'jitterbug' craze.

Then he asked to see me home and that's how I met my future husband, Frank.'

Ted Hughes lived in Greenhithe, Kent, when he first met his future wife, Maisie, at a dance.

'There were two brothers who found that the Methodist Church in Dartford had a very good youth club. So we suddenly became Methodists. There was a boys' club and a girls' club, because you didn't mix in those days. We only mixed at the Christmas dance and that's when I first met Maisie. I took one girl to the youth club party – a girl called Jean – and I took Maisie home!'

Tom Ellis, from Erith in Kent, had similar motives.

'I used to go to dances at Christchurch Hall and the Embassy in Welling, but I wasn't a dancer at all. I would go with the boys to try and chat up the girls. It was all good clean fun and there was never any booze at these places.'

THE THEATRE

The dread of having thousands of people packed into cinemas and theatres up and down the country falling prey to Nazi bombs led the British government to close most venues at the outbreak of war, although they were soon reopened to help maintain the morale of the general public. Few shows in British theatres, however, had the sort of impact enjoyed by Rogers and Hammerstein's *South Pacific*, which opened in 1949. Mary Martin is seen opposite washing that man right out of her hair on Broadway.

GLOBE
THEATRE
LICENSEE & MANAGER: HAROLD GOSLING

6^D

TUPPENCE
COLOURED

NORTHAMPTON

REPERTORY
THEATRE

Monday, June 18th, 1945

In association with C.E.M.A.
THE PILGRIM PLAYERS
present

Murder in the Cathedral

1

THE FORTIES
Good Times Just Around The Corner

everybody would pull away and watch him. He never put a foot wrong. He had the same partner and he used to put her through his legs then spin her up on to his back and she would come down facing him. It was brilliant.'

Paisley-born Mac Black was at a boarding school in Suffolk when the new dance craze took off.

'In the late forties I was into jazz. I loved Louis Armstrong , Bix Beiderbeck and all the musicians who were playing jazz. Every Saturday night, the older pupils would put on the records up in the common room. We all learned to jitterbug and dance and it was fantastic. It was a co-educational school so we didn't dance with boys, because we had girls there. I had some nice relationships there, my first passions – the kind when you think the world is coming to an end when they won't have anything more to do with you!'

Some of the lads still managed to misbehave, as Gerry Maloney admits.

'There used to be a ceilidh, every Sunday night, in the old school hall which had been bombed so it was half a hall. I went with a big gang of friends and we used to get thrown out every week for swinging the girls off their feet, but we would always be let in again the week after.'

The late forties saw a new dance craze sweep through the country. The 'jitterbug' had originated in the United States after Cab Calloway coined the phrase to describe a fast jaunty beat in 1934. The dance, which was similar to a jive, was the in thing for teenagers to learn – but it wasn't that easy, according to Gerry Maloney.

'We were into the suits and the music, but I could never do the dancing. There was a guy I went to school with who was brilliant at it and when we used to go up to the drill hall on Saturday night, he would start dancing and

Left: A GI jives with a WAAF at a 1943 dance.
Below: The Andrews Sisters' upbeat songs were ideal dance tunes.
Opposite: Humphrey Bogart and Ingrid Bergman in Casablanca.

Cinema

Although some picture houses closed down at the beginning of the Second World War, they soon reopened to provide some escape for the beleaguered population of Britain, and they were popular. When the Blitz first began, some attendances did fall, but the audiences soon came flooding back and some cinemas offered shelter for the night. In fact, the amount spent on visits to the cinema and theatre doubled during the war years, and by 1946 a third of the population was going to the cinema at least once a week.

Hollywood dominated the screens with actors such as Ingrid Bergman, Humphrey Bogart, Charlie Chaplin and Bette Davis becoming huge stars, as well as a few home-grown Hollywood exports such as Laurence Olivier and Vivien Leigh.

Classic films of the forties include *Gone with the Wind, Casablanca, Citizen Kane, Mildred Pierce, Brief Encounter* and *The Third Man*. At the same time the British film industry was concentrating on morale-boosting movies depicting the activities of our brave boys in battle, although they didn't always do it the government way. Noël Coward's 1942 classic *In Which We Serve* was based on the experiences of Lord Mountbatten, but was opposed by the Ministry of Information as 'bad propaganda'. After an appeal from Mountbatten to his cousin, the King, it was released and went on to win a special Academy Award.

In 1947, as Britain faced an economic crisis, the Chancellor of the Exchequer put a tax on imported films which so enraged the Motion Picture Association of America that they suspended all shipments of films to the UK. The British film industry seized the opportunity to fill the gap with varying degrees of success. Among the best were the Ealing Studio comedies such as *Whisky Galore, Passport to Pimlico* and *Kind Hearts and Coronets*.

Tom Ellis remembers his nights out at the pictures.

'You went to see a film, but first you would get the Pathé newsreel, then cartoons, then forthcoming attractions, a B-film and travel. You also had a choice of seats and costs, with the cheap seats at the front.

'Sometimes, you'd be just settling in when a message would flash across the screen saying "The sirens have sounded. Patrons wishing to leave the cinema may do so." But you didn't get your money back! I was watching Humphrey Bogart and Edward G. Robinson and all the gangster films coming from the States. There were English films and towards the end they started pushing all the war films like *In Which We Serve* and *Mrs Miniver*.'

As a child, Maurice Tripp often went to the cinema near his North London home.

'After the war there used to be the Saturday morning cinema club for kids. I used to go to ABC Minors for a sixpence and you'd

get a feature, like Roy Rogers, and a cartoon. *Bambi* was the first film I ever saw. I was very affected by that. It was very sad.

'Most of us didn't have televisions in the forties so the only time we saw news was on the newsreels in cinema with Bob Danvers-Walker as the voice behind it. It was all frightfully "received pronunciation". They would show footage of "Our brave boys". Churchill was my hero at the time. I remember, as an eight-year-old boy, watching Pathé News and seeing him leave 10 Downing Street after the election [in 1945], when he'd been voted out and I was so angry. I couldn't believe my hero had been rejected by the country.'

Gill Cook's first experience of the cinema was not a happy one.

'Walt Disney films were a great favourite when we were growing up, but I had to be taken out of *Pinocchio* because I was so frightened. I was four. And I remember crying a lot in *My Friend Flicka* which was about a horse.'

Above: British singing star Gracie Fields, an honorary captain in the Canadian Army.
Right: John Bull magazine was keen to promote more traditional musical values.

1940S BRITISH PRIME MINISTERS

NEVILLE CHAMBERLAIN Became Prime Minister in May 1937 after the resignation of Stanley Baldwin. Resigned himself in May 1940.

WINSTON CHURCHILL Appointed to lead a coalition government on Chamberlain's resignation, Churchill led Britain through the war years but was voted out of office in July 1945, less than a month before final victory over the Japanese.

CLEMENT ATTLEE Voted in with a landslide Labour majority in 1945, Attlee's government would have a narrow victory in the 1950 General Election before losing power to Churchill and the Tories in 1951.

Both pages: After the war, airlines were keen to promote travel to exotic foreign destinations for those who could afford it, while Butlin's was keen to attract those who couldn't.

Holidays

Travel was severely restricted throughout the decade due to the war and the need to conserve fuel. Even in 1948 it was estimated that only half the population went away from home for their holidays, and in the early part of the decade the war meant that people travelled to see their own evacuated families, while children often came home for the school holidays.

Holidays abroad were almost unheard of in the 1940s, only the very wealthy being able to afford the luxury of foreign travel, but for a lucky few in blighted Britain, there was always a week at the seaside to look forward to.

Dorothy Tripp remembers taking a break from Blitz-torn London to visit her sister in Torquay. A case of 'out of the frying pan . . .'

'My sister Marjorie had been evacuated to Torquay with the Prudential, who she worked

BOOK NOW for SEPT. 22-29

IT'S THAT MAN AGAIN!
AT

Butlin's
FILEY (Near SCARBOROUGH)

LUXURY HOLIDAY CAMP

OCTOBER HOLIDAY BARGAIN—FILEY CAMP REMAINING OPEN END OF OCTOBER with all attractions in full swing, inclusive terms £5:0:0 per week.

Special Visit of **TOMMY HANDLEY** and **FULL ITMA COMPANY**

In addition to all the Butlin Holiday attractions.

For booking forms apply: BUTLINS LTD. (T.B.P.), 439, OXFORD ST.. LONDON. W.1.

SPEND A BRIGHT BRACING WEEK-END
AT
BUTLIN'S
LUXURY HOLIDAY CAMP
FILEY
Near Scarborough

ALL-IN TARIFF **16/-** per day

STAR ATTRACTIONS EVERY SUNDAY.
* * * * *
SEPTEMBER 23rd
TOMMY HANDLEY
and the whole ITMA Company
All the usual Butlin Attractions
Booking forms from Camp Manager, E.A.A., Filey, Yorkshire

for. A lot of the big firms evacuated. The Prudential took the Victoria and Albert Hotel right on the front and their office window looked out over the bay. I went down there with Maurice when he was about two. We were on the beach one day with a friend of mine who was staying there too and the German planes started machine-gunning us on the beach! We had to get the two of our children and lie on top of them to protect them. That was worse than the air raids. I phoned my husband and said, "I can't stand it. I'd rather be in London. I'm coming home.'"

Petrol rationing went on until 1950 and the severe shortage of fuel caused by a bitter winter in 1947 meant that most transport stopped altogether. Shortages in labour and materials after

1940S US PRESIDENTS

FRANKLIN DELANO ROOSEVELT

In November 1932, FDR became the USA's thirty-second President. He was re-elected four years later and in 1940 became the first president ever to be elected for a third four-year term. In November 1944, he was voted in yet again, but died in April 1945 just as war in Europe was drawing to a close.

HARRY S. TRUMAN

As Vice-President, Truman automatically became President when Roosevelt died. He retained the Presidency with a surprise win in the 1948 election but chose not to contest the election of 1952, which was won by General Dwight D Eisenhower.

No. 5689 — Volume 242

PRICE THREE SHILLINGS

The Illustrated London News,
May 1, 1948

THE ILLUSTRATED LONDON NEWS

1923 — THEIR MAJESTIES — 1948

ROYAL SILVER WEDDING NUMBER

PRICE 3s. : BY INLAND POST. 3s. 2½d.

PUBLISHING OFFICE : COMMONWEALTH HOUSE,

Left: The Illustrated London News *celebrates the King and Queen's silver wedding in 1948.*
Right: Prestige car makers Humber made the most of the royal celebrations, too.

the war also meant that new cars were hard to buy. Still, some were prepared to go to any lengths for a holiday, as Ted Hughes confesses.

'Maisie and I bought our first car, a 1932 MG Magna, in 1946 but petrol was still scarce so we couldn't do much driving. We used to hoard the coupons for longer journeys. We went down to Dorset. That was the only time I ever bought black market coupons. I heard that a guy at my company sold coupons so I went to him and he said, "Give me the address of where you are staying in Dorset and I'll send them to you." So we went down and one morning an envelope arrived, unsealed, with these coupons inside. But I was so terrified that I would be found out, I never used them! Everybody used to carry lighter fuel in their car so that, if you ran out of petrol, you could fill the carburettor up and get a few miles further.'

Playing Outside

There were few toys available to forties children but imagination, and the freedom to roam, gave them plenty of things to do, as Kath Jarman remembers.

'We never had toys and never expected anything because there were too many of us. In fact, we used our imagination more. I can remember playing

1947
10 July: Princess Elizabeth is awarded extra clothes ration coupons for her wedding dress. She marries Prince Philip of Greece in November.

Above: Rover was just one of many British car companies to go back into commercial production at the war's end. Opposite: The Jaguar XK120 sports car was unveiled at the 1948 Earl's Court Motor Show. The '120' referred to the car's top speed.

with fuchsia flowers and pretending they were ballerina dolls. We used to lay them all along the wall and play with those. At Hailsham, we played in the fields and we used to go looking for brambles and stuff. In London, we used to play everything in the street. We even used to put a rope right across the road and skip, because you hardly saw cars.'

Gerry Maloney had the streets of South London to play in.

'I was hardly indoors because we were always outside playing in the street. We used to play football in Long Lane, which is now a busy London street. But back then, carts were the only thing that came along and you had plenty of warning they were coming.

'We used to play "Tin Can Copper". You got a tin can, put it on a manhole cover then two teams would throw a ball and try and hit the can. Whoever hit the can then had to run and the other team had to run after you and catch you before you could put the tin back in position. If they caught you you were out.'

Bombsites in the cities and suburbs soon became favourite playgrounds for children, including Tom Ellis.

'I think for a little boy it was an exciting time. I used cut though a park to get to school and you'd find new things – a bomb here, a crater there, bits of aeroplane, stacks of shrapnel and things like that. I never felt afraid.'

Maurice Tripp and his friends spent hours on the bombsites in North London

'The bombsites were wonderful for playing on. We played in these sites for years and actually resented it when someone said they were going to rebuild because that was our playground. We collected shrapnel and all kinds of treasures there.'

There wasn't much in the way of children's entertainment but occasional picnic parties and trips to the funfair provided a special treat. Kath Jarman used to look forward to the annual arrival of the funfair.

'It was quite a treat when the fair came to Hailsham, because it was in the field behind where we lived and we could save up to go on a few rides. We would lay in our beds at night time and listen to all the noise. I remember going on the Big Dipper and a few other things. One of the girls I went to school with in senior school went off with one of the men from the fair and fell pregnant, which was not looked upon kindly in those days!'

BESTSELLERS OF THE FORTIES

Most people in Britain in the 1940s did not have televisions. The radio was the thing that occupied pride of place in the living room before the box with a screen finally began to dominate in the 1950s and, while some radio shows like *Dick Barton* kept the family glued to the set, it was perfectly possible to have music playing and amuse yourself with something else at the same time. With a person, a face, talking to you on television, it seemed almost rude not to pay attention, but it was far easier to ignore the disembodied voice of a radio presenter. How did people amuse themselves while the radio played in the background? They read. Newspapers and magazines were devoured by the million, but people were also reading more books than ever before. As a guide to what people were reading, here are some of the bestselling books of the 1940s.

1940

FICTION

1. *How Green Was My Valley*, Richard Llewellyn
2. *Kitty Foyle*, Christopher Morley
3. *Mrs Miniver*, Jan Struther
4. *For Whom the Bell Tolls*, Ernest Hemingway
5. *The Nazarene*, Sholem Asch
6. *Stars on the Sea*, F. van Wyck Mason
7. *Oliver Wiswell*, Kenneth Roberts
8. *The Grapes of Wrath*, John Steinbeck
9. *Night in Bombay*, Louis Bromfield
10. *The Family*, Nina Fedorova

NONFICTION

1. *I Married Adventure*, Osa Johnson
2. *How to Read a Book*, Mortimer Adler
3. *A Smattering of Ignorance*, Oscar Levant
4. *Country Squire in the White House*, John T. Flynn
5. *Land Below the Wind*, Agnes Newton Keith
6. *American White Paper*, Joseph W. Alsop Jr. and Robert Kintnor
7. *New England: Indian Summer*, Van Wyck Brooks
8. *As I Remember Him*, Hans Zinsser
9. *Days of Our Years*, Pierre van Paassen
10. *Bet It's a Boy*, Betty B. Blunt

1941

FICTION

1. *The Keys of the Kingdom*, A. J. Cronin
2. *Random Harvest*, James Hilton
3. *This Above All*, Eric Knight
4. *The Sun Is My Undoing*, Marguerite Steen
5. *For Whom the Bell Tolls*, Ernest Hemingway
6. *Oliver Wiswell*, Kenneth Roberts
7. *H. M. Pulham, Esquire*, John P. Marquand
8. *Mr and Mrs Cugat*, Isabel Scott Rorick
9. *Saratoga Trunk*, Edna Ferber
10. *Windswept*, Mary Ellen Chase

NONFICTION

1. *Berlin Diary*, William L. Shirer
2. *The White Cliffs*, Alice Duer Miller
3. *Out of the Night*, Jan Valtin
4. *Inside Latin America*, John Gunther
5. *Blood, Sweat and Tears*, Winston S. Churchill
6. *You Can't Do Business With Hitler*, Douglas Miller
7. *Reading I've Liked*, Clifton Fadiman, editor
8. *Reveille in Washington*, Margaret Leech
9. *Exit Laughing*, Irvin S. Cobb
10. *My Sister and I*, Dirk van der Heide

1942

FICTION

1. *The Song of Bernadette*, Franz Werfel
2. *The Moon Is Down*, John Steinbeck
3. *Dragon Seed*, Pearl S. Buck
4. *And Now Tomorrow*, Rachel Field
5. *Drivin' Woman*, Elizabeth Pickett
6. *Windswept*, Mary Ellen Chase
7. *The Robe*, Lloyd C. Douglas
8. *The Sun Is My Undoing*, Marguerite Steen
9. *King's Row*, Henry Bellamann
10. *The Keys of the Kingdom*, A. J. Cronin

NONFICTION

1. *See Here, Private Hargrove*, Marion Hargrove
2. *Mission to Moscow*, Joseph E. Davies
3. *The Last Time I Saw Paris*, Elliot Paul
4. *Cross Creek*, Marjorie Kinnan Rawlings
5. *Victory Through Air Power*, Major Alexander P. de Seversky
6. *Past Imperfect*, Ilka Chase
7. *They Were Expendable*, W. L. White
8. *Flight to Arras*, Antoine de St-Exupéry
9. *Washington Is Like That*, W. M. Kiplinger
10. *Inside Latin America*, John Gunther

1943

FICTION

1. *The Robe*, Lloyd C. Douglas
2. *The Valley of Decision*, Marcia Davenport
3. *So Little Time*, John P. Marquand
4. *A Tree Grows in Brooklyn*, Betty Smith
5. *The Human Comedy*, William Saroyan
6. *Mrs Parkington*, Louis Bromfield
7. *The Apostle*, Sholem Asch
8. *Hungry Hill*, Daphne du Maurier
9. *The Forest and the Fort*, Hervey Allen
10. *The Song of Bernadette*, Franz Werfel

NONFICTION

1. *Under Cover*, John Roy Carlson
2. *One World*, Wendell L. Willkie
3. *Journey Among Warriors*, Eve Curie
4. *On Being a Real Person*, Harry Emerson Fosdick
5. *Guadalcanal Diary*, Richard Tregaskis
6. *Burma Surgeon*, Lt-Col. Gordon Seagrave
7. *Our Hearts Were Young and Gay*, Cornelia Otis Skinner and Emily Kimbrough
8. *US Foreign Policy*, Walter Lippmann
9. *Here Is Your War*, Ernie Pyle
10. *See Here, Private Hargrove*, Marion Hargrove

1944

FICTION

1. *Strange Fruit*, Lillian Smith
2. *The Robe*, Lloyd C. Douglas
3. *A Tree Grows in Brooklyn*, Betty Smith
4. *Forever Amber*, Kathleen Winsor
5. *The Razor's Edge*, W. Somerset Maugham
6. *The Green Years*, A. J. Cronin
7. *Leave Her to Heaven*, Ben Ames Williams
8. *Green Dolphin Street*, Elizabeth Goudge
9. *A Bell for Adano*, John Hersey
10. *The Apostle*, Sholem Asch

NONFICTION

1. *I Never Left Home*, Bob Hope
2. *Brave Men*, Ernie Pyle
3. *Good Night*, Sweet Prince, Gene Fowler
4. *Under Cover*, John Roy Carlson
5. *Yankee from Olympus*, Catherine Drinker Bowen
6. *The Time for Decision*, Sumner Welles
7. *Here Is Your War*, Ernie Pyle
8. *Anna and the King of Siam*, Margaret Landon
9. *The Curtain Rises*, Quentin Reynolds
10. *Ten Years in Japan*, Joseph C. Grew

1945

FICTION

1. *Forever Amber*, Kathleen Winsor
2. *The Robe*, Lloyd C. Douglas
3. *The Black Rose*, Thomas B. Costain
4. *The White Tower*, James Ramsey Ullman
5. *Cass Timberlane*, Sinclair Lewis
6. *A Lion Is in the Streets*, Adria Locke Langley
7. *So Well Remembered*, James Hilton
8. *Captain from Castile*, Samuel Shellabarger
9. *Earth and High Heaven*, Adria Locke Langley
10. *Immortal Wife*, Irving Stone

NONFICTION

1. *Brave Men*, Ernie Pyle
2. *Dear Sir*, Juliet Lowell
3. *Up Front*, Bill Mauldin
4. *Black Boy*, Richard Wright
5. *Try and Stop Me*, Bennett Cerf
6. *Anything Can Happen*, George and Helen Papashvily
7. *General Marshall's Report*, US War Department General Staff
8. *The Egg and I*, Betty MacDonald
9. *The Thurber Carnival*, James Thurber
10. *Pleasant Valley*, Louis Bromfield

1946

FICTION

1. *The King's General*, Daphne du Maurier
2. *This Side of Innocence*, Taylor Caldwell
3. *The River Road*, Frances Parkinson Keyes
4. *The Miracle of the Bells*, Russell Janney
5. *The Hucksters*, Frederic Wakeman
6. *The Foxes of Harrow*, Frank Yerby
7. *Arch of Triumph*, Erich Maria Remarque
8. *The Black Rose*, Thomas B. Costain
9. *B. F.'s Daughter*, John P. Marquand
10. *The Snake Pit*, Mary Jane Ward

NONFICTION

1. *The Egg and I*, Betty MacDonald
2. *Peace of Mind*, Joshua L. Liebman
3. *As He Saw It*, Elliott Roosevelt
4. *The Roosevelt I Knew*, Frances Perkins
5. *Last Chapter*, Ernie Pyle
6. *Starling of the White House*, Thomas Sugrue and Col. Edmund Starling
7. *I Chose Freedom*, Victor Kravchenko
8. *The Anatomy of Peace*, Emery Reves
9. *Top Secret*, Ralph Ingersoll
10. *A Solo in Tom-Toms*, Gene Fowler

1947

FICTION

1. *The Miracle of the Bells*, Russell Janney
2. *The Moneyman*, Thomas B. Costain
3. *Gentleman's Agreement*, Laura Z. Hobson
4. *Lydia Bailey*, Kenneth Roberts
5. *The Vixens*, Frank Yerby
6. *The Wayward Bus*, John Steinbeck
7. *House Divided*, Ben Ames Williams
8. *Kingsblood Royal*, Sinclair Lewis
9. *East Side, West Side*, Marcia Davenport
10. *Prince of Foxes*, Samuel Shellabarger

NONFICTION

1. *Peace of Mind*, Joshua L. Liebman
2. *Information Please Almanac, 1947*, John Kieran, editor
3. *Inside USA*, John Gunther
4. *A Study of History*, Arnold J. Toynbee
5. *Speaking Frankly*, James F. Byrnes
6. *Human Destiny*, Pierre Lecomte du Noüy
7. *The Egg and I*, Betty MacDonald
8. *The American Past*, Roger Butterfield
9. *The Fireside Book of Folk Songs*, Margaret B. Boni, editor
10. *Together*, Katharine T. Marshall

1948

FICTION

1. *The Big Fisherman*, Lloyd C. Douglas
2. *The Naked and the Dead*, Norman Mailer
3. *Dinner at Antoine's*, Frances Parkinson Keyes
4. *The Bishop's Mantle*, Agnes Sligh Turnbull
5. *Tomorrow Will Be Better*, Betty Smith
6. *The Golden Hawk*, Frank Yerby
7. *Raintree County*, Ross Lockridge Jr
8. *Shannon's Way*, A. J. Cronin
9. *Pilgrim's Inn*, Elizabeth Goudge
10. *The Young Lions*, Irwin Shaw

NONFICTION

1. *Crusade in Europe*, Dwight D. Eisenhower
2. *How to Stop Worrying and Start Living*, Dale Carnegie
3. *Peace of Mind*, Joshua L. Liebman
4. *Sexual Behavior in the Human Male*, A. C. Kinsey, *et al.*
5. *Wine, Women and Words*, Billy Rose
6. *The Life and Times of the Shmoo*, Al Capp
7. *The Gathering Storm*, Winston Churchill
8. *Roosevelt and Hopkins*, Robert E. Sherwood
9. *A Guide to Confident Living*, Norman Vincent Peale
10. *The Plague and I*, Betty MacDonald

1949

FICTION

1. *The Egyptian*, Mika Waltari
2. *The Big Fisherman*, Lloyd C. Douglas
3. *Mary*, Sholem Asch
4. *A Rage to Live*, John O'Hara
5. *Point of No Return*, John P. Marquand
6. *Dinner at Antoine's*, Frances Parkinson Keyes
7. *High Towers*, Thomas B. Costain
8. *Cutlass Empire*, Van Wyck Mason
9. *Pride's Castle*, Frank Yerby
10. *Father of the Bride*, Edward Streeter

NONFICTION

1. *White Collar Zoo*, Clare Barnes Jr
2. *How to Win at Canasta*, Oswald Jacoby
3. *The Seven Storey Mountain*, Thomas Merton
4. *Home Sweet Zoo*, Clare Barnes Jr
5. *Cheaper by the Dozen*, Frank B. Gilbreth Jr and Ernestine Gilbreth Carey
6. *The Greatest Story Ever Told*, Fulton Oursler
7. *Canasta, the Argentine Rummy Game*, Ottilie H. Reilly
8. *Canasta*, Josephine Artayeta de Viel and Ralph Michael
9. *Peace of Soul*, Fulton J. Sheen
10. *A Guide to Confident Living*, Norman Vincent Peale

CHAPTER SIX

SPORTS AND HOBBIES

There was very little sport played while the war in Europe continued, as many of the country's sportsmen had been called up. After the war, however, sport proved more popular than ever, providing an inexpensive diversion from the drudgery of post-war living.

Spectator Sports

In the run up to World War II, encouraged by the Football Association who urged teams to set a patriotic example to the country's youth, most footballers had joined the Territorial Army and other national-service organizations, such as the War Reserve Police. As the call-up papers started to go out, the professional teams found themselves without many of their star players and scrabbling to put together a decent side. Travel was also restricted, so bussing a London team to Yorkshire for an important match was impossible. As a result, the sport was split into eight geographical groups, each with its own league. The players were allowed to be paid no more than 30 shillings for each match and, for safety reasons, no more than 8,000 spectators were allowed in the ground.

Gerry Maloney spent his Saturdays at Millwall during the war, and remembers one remarkable opponent.

'Millwall carried on playing during the war

Previous pages – Left: Dutch athlete Fanny Blankers-Koen was the star of the 1948 Olympics, winning four gold medals. Right: Official programme from the 1948 Olympics in London. Below: The Dynamo Moscow team walks out onto the pitch at Chelsea's Stamford Bridge ground on 13 November 1945 carrying flowers for their opponents.

and they used to play Aldershot. Because they were a team from the army barracks they had the pick of the army which included Frank Swift, the England goalkeeper. They had Mercer, Cullis and Britton who were the English half line and they had Dave McCulloch, a Scottish International and Jimmy Hagan, an English International, in the forward line so they were a powerful side and they used to slaughter everybody. They were brilliant.

'Millwall used to have a little guy called Granger, from Leeds, who was a fast winger but he was only little. He used to charge Frank Swift, this massive goalkeeper, who would lift the ball over his head like he wasn't there.

'It was always easy to get in and there was no seating. There was no trouble either. People weren't segregated but it was all treated as a laugh and dads could take their kids because it never got nasty.'

Harry Bridges was growing up in Fencehouses, County Durham.

'Football was still an important part of wartime life. I can remember being taken to Sunderland's ground, Roker Park, by my father and the train being so full that the young boys were seated on the luggage racks. I was often lifted over the turnstile, so I got in free. I have vivid memories of seeing a wartime International (England v. Scotland) at Newcastle and had my first sighting of such legends as Stanley Matthews, Tommy Lawton and Stan Mortensen.'

The end of the war brought new interest in football and the grounds saw the highest attendance ever. Harry faithfully followed his favourite side.

'Along with my school mates it became a fortnightly pilgrimage to Roker Park. Crowds were large as supporters made up for lost time. At one cup match there were so many that they charged across the pitch to occupy a stand that had been closed for use as a storage facility during the war. My regular

Stanley Matthews was one of the most influential players of the 1940s and is seen here playing in the FA cup final at the age of 38 in 1953. He wouldn't eventually retire from first class football until he was 50!

Saturday became match, fish-and-chip tea in town and then home on the train.

'We all had our own heroes and I remember rushing to the local CWS Co-op on hearing they had a delivery of Stan Matthews autographed boots (they didn't work – I didn't get any better!) While we played our own games we all pretended to be one of the day's greats, depending on who we supported.'

In 1945 British football fans were in for a rare treat when Moscow Dynamo came to the UK to take on four of the top clubs. Gerry Maloney was at one of the historic matches.

'The most amazing game I saw was at Stamford Bridge when the Moscow Dynamos

Left: The ballpoint pen was one invention from the 1940s that had an immediate effect on almost everyone.
Right: Brylcreem was just the thing, as this advertisement says, for athletes and sportsmen because it 'controls the hair perfectly during the most vigorous exercise.'

came over to play Chelsea. It was the first foreign team to come over and they were stunning. There were so many people there that they lifted the kids over the heads of the crowds and put them down the front, round the edge of the pitch. It was packed because nobody had ever seen anything like that.'

Cricket also suffered during the war, with many grounds being requisitioned for wartime use. The Oval, for instance, was used as a prisoner-of-war camp. Test matches were cancelled and didn't resume until 1946 when, like football, cricket began to enjoy the highest attendances ever.

The Australians, led by the great Don Bradman, dominated the game at international level and demonstrated their skills on a five-Test tour of England in 1948. The England team could boast such legends as Len Hutton and Dennis Compton.

Cricket was Harry Bridges's passion when he was growing up in the North-East.

'Durham was only classed as a minor county so I passed my allegiance on to Yorkshire and had many enjoyable days watching matches at the Scarborough Cricket Festival. I was also lucky enough to visit Headingley to watch Test matches. In the war years I can remember watching an Australian services XI, including the great Keith Miller, at Ashbrooke in Sunderland. Most of the team were past and future Australian Test players.'

Ted Hughes shared a love of cricket with his father.

'Cricket was my thing. I used to go to county matches all the time. My father was a good cricketer and he used to play in the Minor Counties League, and I was quite good. I saw Denis Compton play as well as Don

Men of the world prove

BRYLCREEM

the perfect Hair Dressing

● You cannot feel your best unless you look your best—that's why Brylcreem is the world's favourite hair dressing; it supplies the finishing touch to perfect grooming.

Athletes and sportsmen prefer Brylcreem because it controls the hair perfectly during the most vigorous exercise—and its valuable tonic effects keep the scalp in first-class condition.

Business men use Brylcreem because it keeps the hair smartly in position throughout the most hair ruffling day! And a little Brylcreem each morning is a grand insurance against "Dry Hair" and "Tight Scalp" and other hair troubles.

Look after the health of your look your best—look out for Brylcreem, the perfect Hair Dress

NO GUM · NO SOAP
NO SPIRIT · NO STARCH
YES—BRYLCREEM YOUR HAI

County Perfumery Co. Ltd., Honeypot Lane, Stanmore, Middlesex. 26

1948
5 July: Doctors, nurses and other healthcare professionals and hospital staff become state employees under the new National Health Service.

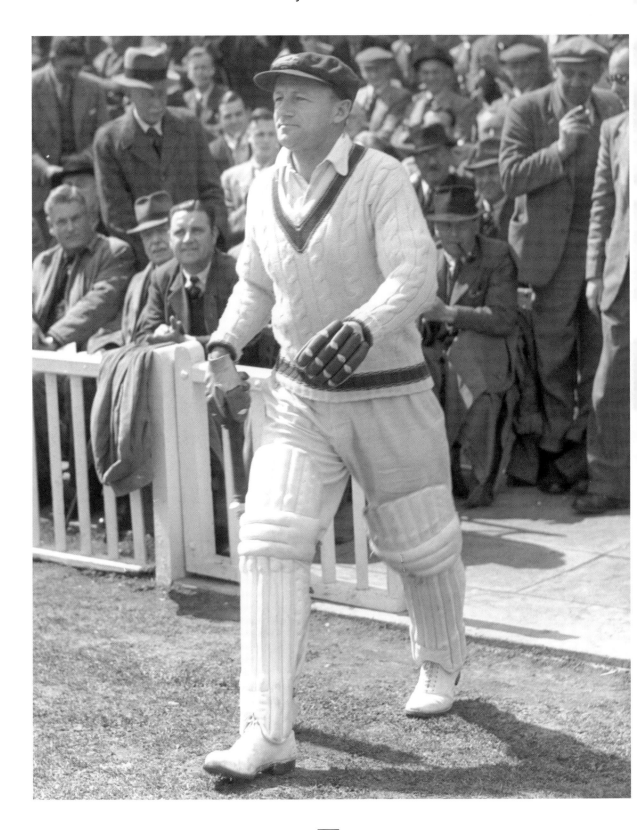

Above: Speedway at Wembley wasn't just a sport for the boys – these young women are cheering on their heroes.
Left: Australian captain Don Bradman goes in to bat at Worcester during his farewell tour in 1948.

Bradman and Len Hutton.

'Bill Bowes, who played for Yorkshire and England and was one of the "Bodyline" bowlers, was a friend of my dad's. Whenever he had a match down here we didn't see my father for days because they would go out on the town.'

The 1948 Australian 'Invincibles' tour also saw Don Bradman's last Test match. Coming into bat to a standing ovation at the Oval, he needed four runs to secure a lifetime test average of 100 runs. Sadly, to the surprise of the crowd, he was bowled by the second ball from England's Eric Hollies and ended his Test career with a duck! His average stayed at 99.94.

Speedway was another sport which inspired massive enthusiasm, generating formidable post-war crowds. Weekly events were held at stadiums around the country and at Wembley, the biggest venue of all, crowds in 1946 typically numbered between 65,000 and 85,000. At one meeting, on 3 October 1946, the number of speedway fans attending was so huge that the stadium gates had

Above: Seen here in practice, Tommy Price was a member of the Wembley Lions speedway team that won the World Championship in 1949.
Right: Giving the world a Coke in 1948.

to be closed with 20,000 more fans outside.

Gerry Maloney was a speedway fan in the forties.

'We used to go to speedway at New Cross after the war. Ron Johnson was the big noise at New Cross stadium, and Split Waterman. A big group of us used to go up there and you used to get medals which you put on your jacket with the year on it and then we'd go every week.'

Joe Louis dominated the boxing ring in the 1940s. Having become Heavyweight Champion of the World in 1937, he held on to the title for twelve years and defended it twenty-five times. In 1949 Louis, known as 'the Brown Bomber', officially retired, although he was to return a year later for a few more fights. Gerry Maloney was also a fan of Louis.

'Joe Louis was a great champion but, unfortunately, I never saw him fight. We used to listen to the big fights on the radio. We watched boxing a lot, but on a more local level. We used to go the local clubs and to watch the shows at the Bermondsey baths where one club would fight another. Some of the lads who boxed there became top international fighters.'

All over the world  *bring...ent*

THE FORTIES
Good Times Just Around The Corner

The 1948 Olympics

After two cancelled Olympics because of the war, the games came to London in 1948. The 1936 Olympics, in Berlin, had been notoriously extravagant and had turned into a propaganda exercise for Adolf Hitler. In stark contrast, the London Olympics, held amid the restrictions of post-war rationing and shortages, were dubbed 'the Austerity Olympics.' The athletes were housed in a number of military camps, colleges and schools. Between twenty-five and thirty sites were used, meaning that transport had to be arranged from there to the various sports grounds.

As it was thought that restricting the diets of the foreign athletes might have a bad psychological

Top: The official souvenir brochure of London's 1948 Olympics.
Below: The Olympic flame arrives in London.
Opposite: Britain's Olympic team had support in all quarters.

OLYMPIC GAMES LONDON 1948 OFFICIAL SOUVENIR

CALLING ALL SPORTSMEN !

Leading sportsmen of
the day wear and acclaim
THE LITESOME SUPPORTER

Another Olympic Games brings fitness to the fore ! Men who keep in championship trim, day after day, year after year, say what they owe to the Litesome Supporter. It's part of their sports equipment that they wouldn't be without. So also with men in every kind of job, from ages of eighteen to eighty !

The Litesome with its effective original features gives that *all-necessary* support at " points of strain." The muscles of the lower abdomen are gently braced and supported. Buoyant uplift is knitted into the fabric of the Litesome Supporter, built into its shape. The Litesome gives that " on top of the world " feeling which is worth points in any sport or job ! Sales of over a million testify to this !

As used by the British Olympic Athletic Team

LITESOME SUPPORTER FOR MEN

STANDARD MODEL 7/6
MAYFAIR MODEL 16/9

Fully distributed through Out-fitters, Sports Shops, Chemists.

If difficulty, C.O.D. (state waist size) from the makers.

LITESOME
ON TOP OF THE WORLD

Overseas Agencies are open! Agencies in many overseas territories for this fine, fast-selling line are still open ! Foreign buyers are invited to write at once to :

FRED HURTLEY LTD., KEIGHLEY, YORKS. Phone : KEIGHLEY 2453
Telegrams and Cables : LITESOME, KEIGHLEY.

" *Wetting one's whistle...* "

To all whistlers whether instrumentalists or otherwise, whistle wetting is an essential part of the joy of life. And everyone agrees that there's nothing better than a glass of cool refreshing Kia-Ora for hitting the right note. Yes! Kia-Ora is delicious always!

MAKE A QUICK GETAWAY FROM **COLDS**

by using . . .

POTTER'S

CATARRH PASTILLES

POTTER & CLARKE LTD, ARTILLERY LANE, E·I

Above; Catarrh pastilles were the ideal thing to keep you tubes clear . . .
Left: . . . while Kia-Ora was just the thing to wet your whistle.

effect they were given 'Category A' meal allowances – the allowance for heavy workers such as coal miners and dockers – but with the addition of two pints of milk per day and half a pound of chocolates and sweets per week. Due to the shortages, however, the 'gold' medals were made from oxidized silver.

The Americans dominated the track and field events, bagging thirty-eight gold medals, and although Britain failed to win a single gold for athletics, the home nation came first in rowing and yachting events. The most memorable athlete, however, was a female Dutch runner called Fanny Blankers-Koen. The thirty-year-old mother of two,

known as 'the Flying Dutchwoman', took the gold in four track events.

Terry Millner travelled from Oxford to join the massive crowd at Wembley.

'I remember the tracks because they were covered with cinder which, apparently, came from the fireplaces of Leicester. Because we were still suffering the after-effects of the war, it was wonderful to be at such a memorable event and the atmosphere was terrific. I was thrilled to see Emil Zatopek, the Czech runner, because he set a new record in the 10,000 metres. It was very exciting.'

1949
25 October: The price of a gallon of petrol goes up to 2s 3d (11p), equivalent nowadays to about 2.5 pence per litre.

ii

EXPERIENCE
makes them the Greatest
Names in Cycling

* Patent Dyno-Luxe lighting, patent built-in thief-proof lock, stainless steel rims and spokes, alloy fittings, special finish and many exclusive features in design. Visit your local Dealer and ask him for Catalogues.

Established
1887 RALEIGH
1869 RUDGE
1886 HUMBER
1903 STURMEY-ARCHER

Made and built throughout in the largest and most modern cycle plant in the World

PRODUCTS OF RALEIGH INDUSTRIES LIMITED, NOTTINGHAM

C.B.H.9F

Left: British bicycles were back in manufacture by 1949 and more popular than ever.
Opposite: The Land Rover was launched at the Amsterdam Motor Show in 1948 and is still going strong today.

countries took part. For the girls there was the Girl Guides, which enjoyed growing popularity in the late forties with worldwide membership exceeding 3 million by the early 1950s.

The Young Farmers' Club was another success, with 65,000 members in 1946, and other clubs revolved around such activities as football or boxing. In 1949 over 200,000 schoolboys belonged to the National Association of Boys' Clubs.

Tom Ellis remembers a few clubs in his hometown of Erith, Kent.

'The main social life was sitting around at the Boys' Club, the church club and the youth club and then I was in to the theatre. The amateur-dramatics clubs in our area were very strong after the war. I started when I was sixteen. Scouts were also a big thing. They were very strong during and after the war. Many of the Scout leaders were away during the war so younger people, like myself, were running the troops.

'There wasn't any television so you had to do something else, so you belonged to clubs like Scouts and Cubs and you went out in the evening.

Clubs
Clubs and associations swiftly grew in popularity after the war with youth centres opening up everywhere, largely as an attempt to keep youngsters away from the dirty and dangerous bombsites. The Boy Scouts enjoyed a record attendance with its membership swelling to 470,000 by 1949. In 1947 the Sixth World Jamboree of Boy Scouts, named 'The Jamboree of Peace', was held in France and scouts from fifty

'I remember coming home from the youth club about ten o'clock and the overhead cables for the trolley bus were down so it couldn't move, so a few of us pushed the trolley bus over the hill so that it could get connected again.'

Gerry Maloney belonged to his local club at Dockhead, South London.

'We had one club for 11-14 year-olds, one for 14-18 and then there was the Fisher Club which I belonged to. The Fisher Club had been going since 1903 but it was really popular in the forties. It was a football club but we did box as well. I fought for them four times. I won the first fight – I stopped an Irish Guardsman – but I lost the next two fights.

'We went down to "camp" on holidays as a club, too. It was a site near Worth Priory, in Sussex, where we slept in either the bunkhouse, which had lots of beds in it, or in tents. There was a cookhouse and a little wooden chapel and we would get up in the morning and wash with freezing cold water from two buckets. During the day we would go swimming or walking or play football, and in the evening we would go to a local

dance. We had a great time there.

'There weren't many clubs around for the girls. Once a week, on a Thursday night, they were allowed to go to the Fisher Club but the boys weren't there that night.'

Through the rise of television and home computers clubs were, eventually, to lose their popularity, but for teenagers in the 1940s they were a way of life.

EPILOGUE

Although the Second World War had left the country in economic strife, the austerity of the war and post-war years was just beginning to ease by the end of the decade. The American aid programme, named 'the Marshall Plan' after Secretary of State George C. Marshall, saw $13.3 billion distributed between sixteen European countries immediately after the war, and by the end of the decade things were beginning to look up.

Although most rationing continued into the fifties, with meat the last item to drop off the ration book in 1954, clothes were not restricted after 1949. Youngsters had a brief glimpse of heaven when rationing for sweets and chocolates ended, temporarily, in April 1949, only to be reinstated in August!

In 1947 Deputy Prime Minister Herbert Morrison (who gave his name to the Morrison shelter) announced plans for the 'Festival of Britain' which was to take place in 1951, to boost the morale of the nation. As well as a travelling exhibition of concerts, firework displays and other events, 27 acres of derelict, bomb-damaged ground on the south bank of the River Thames in London were to be used to build halls and theatres. The idea, described by Morrison as 'the people giving themselves a pat on the back,' had its opponents, who argued that the nation's economy had not yet recovered enough for a national celebration. But for the ordinary people of Britain, beleaguered and wearied by the restraints of post-war rationing, the idea of a party for the whole country went some way to changing the mood and raising optimism.

The 1940s had been a time of hardship, heartache and heroism. The next decade was to be a time of consumerism and relative prosperity, with everyday chores made easier as the refrigerator became a standard requirement and the washing machine began to replace the dolly tub and mangle. The television was about to replace the radio as the major source of home entertainment and cars were to become an affordable necessity rather than a luxury.

As the forties drew to a close the plans for the Festival of Britain captured the mood of the nation, and the growing feeling that good times were just around the corner.

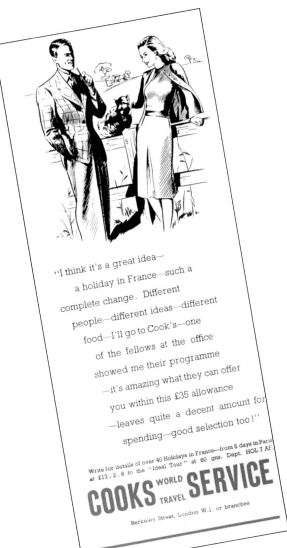

"I think it's a great idea—a holiday in France—such a complete change. Different people—different ideas—different food—I'll go to Cook's—one of the fellows at the office showed me their programme—it's amazing what they can offer you within this £35 allowance—leaves quite a decent amount for spending—good selection too!"

Write for details of over 40 Holidays in France—from 5 days in Paris at £13 . 2 . 6 to the "Ideal Tour" at 60 gns. Dept. HOL 7 AF

COOKS WORLD TRAVEL SERVICE

Berkeley Street, London W.1. or branches

Left: There were restrictions on the amount of money you could take out of the country when you went on holiday in the late 1940s . . .
Right: . . . but no longer any constraints on the amount of make-up you could use!

GLAMOUR *maxfactorized*

DEBORAH KERR
M G M Star of
"IF WINTER COMES"

It's so easy to be *maxfactorized* . . . so exciting and thrilling. too. Just try this famous *Max Factor Hollywood* Make-up in the correct shades which are individually prescribed to enliven, enhance, and harmonize perfectly with the natural colourings of your hair, eyes and complexion . . . and you will be transformed, as if by magic, into a vision of irresistible loveliness.

COLOUR HARMONY MAKE-UP

MAX FACTOR Cosmetics of the Stars' are obtainable from your local Chemist, Hair-dresser & Store

created by

Max Factor
HOLLYWOOD & LONDON